UITGAVEN VAN HET
NEDERLANDS HISTORISCH-ARCHAEOLOGISCH INSTITUUT TE ISTANBUL

Publications de l'Institut historique et archéologique néerlandais de Stamboul
sous la direction de
E. VAN DONZEL, Machteld J. MELLINK,
C. NIJLAND et J.J. ROODENBERG

XLVII

THE BAHRAIN TUMULI
AN ILLUSTRATED CATALOGUE OF TWO IMPORTANT COLLECTIONS

THE BAHRAIN TUMULI

AN ILLUSTRATED CATALOGUE OF TWO IMPORTANT COLLECTIONS

by

ELISABETH C.L. DURING CASPERS

NEDERLANDS HISTORISCH-ARCHAEOLOGISCH INSTITUUT
TE ISTANBUL
1980

I.S.B.N. 90 6258 047 5
Printed in Belgium

To my parents
With gratitude

TABLE OF CONTENTS

INTRODUCTION

Contrary to the statement in *Persica VI* 1972-1974[1] that a detailed catalogue of the Jefferson and Higham grave mound material from Bahrain would appear in *Persica VII* 1974-1975[2], this project did not materialize. I am, therefore, grateful to "Het Nederlands Historisch-Archaeologisch Instituut te Istanbul" for offering me the opportunity to publish this extensive photographic documentation in its present form.

It is neither the intention of this photographic catalogue to offer up to date parallels and references for the material under discussion, be it prehistoric, Parthian or Roman, nor to provide the reader with a further updated recording of the cultural periods to which the various grave objects themselves belong. The previous paper already published in *Persica VI* 1972-1974 has already provided an abreviated account of the comparisons and parallels, which were available at that time.

The simple aim of this catalogue is to illustrate adequately each of the items discovered and reported by Mrs. E.P. Jefferson and Captain R. Higham R.S., and to record the observations noted down by these two amateur archaeologists in the process of their work. These details, subsequently passed on to me, I intend to reproduce here, as it were, *verbatim*. In these circumstances, I must therefore abdicate at the outset from any responsibility regarding the possibility of inaccuracies relating to the precise location of the findspots — a common hazard when dealing with illegal explorations — together with faulty interpretation and incorrect recordings. These may well contradict the observations published or noted by others, whether they be amateurs or professional archaeologists.

However, in spite of the lapse of time between the date of appearance of the paper in *Persica VI* 1972-1974 and the present publication, the statement which appeared in the latter (p. 135), is still relevant "Although these tumuli were excavated by amateurs it is thought that the objects found, are of sufficient importance to the history of Bahrain to warrant their publication." Rapid industrial development, and the consequential risks to archaeological traces and material, are

[1] I am much indebted to the Netherlands Organization for the Advancement of Pure Research for their financial support which enabled me to study these two collections at the British Museum, London, and additionally, Parthian pottery at the Institute of Archaeology, University of Turin, Italy and at the Musée du Louvre, Paris, France.

[2] Elisabeth C.L. During Caspers, The Bahrain tumuli, *Persica VI* 1972-1974 (1974), pp. 131-156; see also ID., The Bahrain Tumuli, *Proceedings of the Seminar for Arabian Studies* 2 1972 (formerly Proceedings of the Fifth Seminar for Arabian Studies, 1971 (1972)), pp. 9-19.

prevalent in most parts of the world. Bahrain is presently contending with this problem in the restricted fertile acreage of the island, and it is possible that the archaeologist may be faced with an outcome where the Dilmun of the past, so eloquently described by its Sumerian contemporaries, may be doomed to remain an ill-glimpsed ghost, overtaken by modern ventures.

The funerary objects from the tumulus at Hamala North in Central Bahrain, opened by Mrs. E.P. Jefferson in 1968, were in 1969, before the passing of the present law of antiquities, generously presented by the excavator to the Department of Western Asiatic Antiquities of the British Museum, London.

Although this latter grave furniture is by far the smaller of the two collections under discussion, its importance is twofold. On the one hand the variety of objects found together in this one grave, can in most cases be parallelled elsewhere, whether within or outside the grave mound horizon. As such, it forms a useful basis for comparative and chronological purposes. On the other hand, one must take account of the presence of pieces so far unparallelled, as for instance the copper/bronze stem-footed goblet, the upper part of a reddish clay goblet with a dark plum-red decoration, and a tiny copper/bronze horned animal which has a loop-attachment.

Captain R. Higham's grave objects, which come from 23 graves situated at different localities on the island of Bahrain and cover more than one cultural period, are far more extensive and are, in fact, quite unique because of the variety of fine, glazed Parthian pottery, some of which was deposited in the same grave as three exquisite Roman glass vessels, which latter can provide a secure date in the second half of the first century A.D.

So far no definite steps appear to have been taken to preserve the important Higham collection [3], which was also taken out of Bahrain before the present law on antiquities, and which rests at present on deposit with the Department of Western Asiatic Antiquities of the British Museum. We may well have to face the fatal possibility of an ultimate dispersion of these various objects. This fact in itself demands a detailed and well illustrated report, and the reader will, therefore, often find more than one photograph of the same object.

[3] I wish to express my indebtedness to Dr. R.D. Barnett, former Keeper of the Department of Western Asiatic Antiquities, to Dr. E. Sollberger, present Keeper of the above mentioned department of the British Museum and to Mr. T. Mitchell, Deputy Keeper of this department for their kind co-operation and assistance on many occasions, during the time I worked on this material, and for their generous gesture in housing the Higham collection over the past years. My sincere thanks are also due to Mr. C. Bateman and Mr. J. Bateman for cleaning, treating and analysing this material in the laboratory of the British Museum, to Lady Jane Cook and Miss R. Enderly for drawing most of the material, and to Mr. C. May, at that time photographer at the British Museum and to Mrs. J.C.M.H. Moloney for doing the photography.

JEFFERSON TUMULUS — HAMALA NORTH

Figs. 1, 2 a-d, 3 a, 4 b, Plates III-VII

The grave consisted of a main burial chamber with two adjoining open alcoves, one at the north side, the other at the south side of the eastern section of the main chamber. The funerary gifts, accompanying the deceased were found in the southern section of the main burial chamber (see Tables I-II).

Fig. 2 b, Plate III 1-2

Against the south wall stood a round-bodied "cooking pot" with slightly pointed base, no neck and a tiny rim which is slightly convex on the outside and concave on the inside. It was made of a brownish-red, grit-tempered, brittle clay showing small white speckles of the type referred to as "exploding white grits" on the outer and inner surface. There are traces of burning on the lower part as well as on the inside. The slightly pointed base is burnt blackish. There is no slip, but this thin-walled, brittle pot shows traces of wet-smoothing as can be clearly demonstrated by the "dripping impressions" under the rim. Moreover, there are indications that at least the lower part was hand-made. The height of this "cooking pot" is 0.17,1 metres, the diameter of the rim measures 0.12,3 metres and the rim is 0.003-0.004 metres thick.

Fig. 2c, Plate V 1-2

Next to the above "cooking pot," rested the upper part of a wheel-thrown goblet with thin walls, made of a brick-red coloured clay, which originally may have had a pedestalled splayed foot since identifiable fragments were present. The fabric is well levigated and the goblet is well fired. Due to the high salt percentage of the soil inside the tumulus, the outer surface of both slip and plum-red decoration is seen to be flaking off rather extensively.

The entire outer surface had been covered with a slip which, where it survives, is of a red colour, with the exception of one portion of the upper part of the goblet where this slip is whitish-buff. It has been suggested that the entire slip may have been intended to be finished as a whitish buff, but since its application was significantly uneven, only that portion of the upper part of the goblet where the slip was thick enough, acquired the desired colour. The remainder of the goblet, where the white slip was too thinly applied retained its underlying colour. However, it cannot be conclusively certain that the condition of the soil inside in the tumulus does not have its own bearing upon these colour differences.

A dark plum-red decoration was applied on the inside of the unslipped rim as well as on the slipped outer surface and it forms a zone on the upper part of the goblet closed off above and below by solid plum-red paint.

This zone, approximately 0.03,7 metres in width, contains five cross-hatched butterfly motifs, also in plum-red, each wing measuring 0.01,5-0.02,5 metres across and interspersed at one point for a width of 0.05 metres, by a tree motif (?) with clusters of leaves (?) hanging down on either side of the central stem. Below this zone, the plum-red paint covers the lower portion of the goblet and it would appear also the stem and the splayed foot. This can be surmised fairly conclusively by the presence of slightly hollow, splayed foot fragments, made of the same brick-red clay as the goblet top and covered by the same plum-red paint. The present height of the broken goblet is 0.09,1 metres, the diameter of the rim measures 0.11,7 metres and the height of the actual foot can be reconstructed as ca. 0.003 metres, although the height of the stem cannot be ascertained.

Fig. 3 a, Plate IV 2

Also placed against the south wall of the main burial chamber and to the east of the latter two vessels, lay a pear-shaped, thin-walled jar with a small sagging base, a short straight neck and a simple out-turned rim. It is made of a dirty-cream coloured clay with a greenish tinge and is well-fired. There is no slip, but the jar was probably wet-smoothed. Two shallow ridges in relief run around the top of the shoulder. Although the rim and the upper shoulder give the impression of having been thrown on a wheel, the lower part of this jar seems to have been modelled by hand, this being especially noticeable near the base. This combined technique of throwing the neck and the upper shoulder on a wheel and forming the lower portion by hand, recurs in the red pear-shaped pottery found by Captain Higham (Fig. 4c-e, Plates VIII-IX, XIV-XV). The height is 0.40,5 metres and the diameter of the rim measures 0.13,8 metres.

Fig. 2 a, Plate IV 1

Towards the west wall of the main burial chamber stood a thin-walled oval-shaped jar with a roundish, pointed sagging base, a sharply carinated, almost horizontally inturned shoulder, a short vertical neck and a flat-topped, everted rim. It is made of a pale reddish-buff clay, well levigated, with a whithish-cream slip and appears to be well-fired and wheel-thrown. Repair holes at the junction of the rim and the neck, show that this jar had already been mended in antiquity. The height is 0.21 metres and the diameter of the rim measures 0.15,4 metres.

Plate VII 1

Also towards the west wall of the main burial chamber lay a substantial base fragment of a flat-based "flower pot" with walls tapering obliquely outwards. The junction of the base and the walls is somewhat rounded off. The fragment is made of a light buff coloured clay which is only slightly darker than the pear-shaped jar with small sagging base of Plate IV 2. There are no traces of a slip and the pot appears to have been wheel-made, with thickened walls of between 0.007-0.01,5 metres. In spite of it being tempered with coarse sand and small crushed particles of gravel, the pot is well-fired. The remaining height is 0.08,5 metres and the diameter of the base measures 0.09,5 metres.

Not illustrated, and without a recorded location within the grave, is a pottery fragment of a buffish, light-brown coloured clay, with on the outside traces of an overall coating of plum-red paint. Three of the four sides are rounded off by wear, the fourth side shows a sharp break as if this fragment originally may have been larger. Its most conceivable use appears to be as a rubber for smoothing pottery when still wet. The remaining length is 0.09,7 metres, the width 0.07,5 metres.

Fig. 2d, Plate VI 1-2

Left of the skull and close against the east wall of the burial chamber was a copper/bronze rimless goblet on a short, hollow, cylindrical stem and a splayed hollow foot, which has a concave base. The metal has an average thickness of 0.001 metres. The beaker-shaped upper portion of this goblet is in a very fragmentary and corroded state. The stem and foot, although fragile due to corrosion, are complete and unbroken. Some stones had been placed on the foot of the vessel, for what purpose is not clear, unless to prevent the goblet from tipping over, in which case it may have contained a liquid. The remains give the impression that the complete vessel may have been somewhat top-heavy. The overall height of this vessel is 0.18 metres, the reconstructed diameter of the rim measures ca. 0.21,5 metres, the height of the stem is 0.04 metres and the diameter of the foot measures 0.07,7-0.07,9 metres.

Fig. 4b, Plate VII 2

In the north-eastern section of the main burial chamber, hard up against the northern wall a copper/bronze pin was discovered. Centrally the pin is fashioned to have a rectangular cross-section, but one end tapers towards a rounded rather blunt point, whilst the other end is somewhat flattened, before also terminating in a point. It measures 0.13,7 metres in length and approximate midway cross-sections measure 0.003 × 0.003-0.003 × 0.005 metres.

Fig. 4b, Plate VII 2

Near the foot end of the northern wall, close to the above mentioned, lay a copper/bronze "omega"—shaped metal object, broken in two places. One break in the middle of the loop appears to be ancient, a second one in the right leg 2/3 down is new and the two ends fit perfectly. The length is 0.05,7 metres, the width measured across at ca. 1/3 of the length is 0.01,8-0.01,9 metres, and the width measured from the tips of the two upturned ends is 0.03,6 metres. The object (a pin?) is ca. 0.04 metres thick [2].

Fig. 4b, Plate VII 2

From the northern section of the main burial chamber there is also a tiny copper/bronze horned animal, probably a goat, in a very corroded state. This minute animal stands on a short base and has been naturally modelled on all aspects. It displays a superior workmanship, especially when one takes into account its small dimensions. A loop-attachment, soldered to one side of the animal about mid-way along its body, suggests that this delightful piece originally served as an ornament or may have formed part of a pin. Its total height is 0.02 metres, the height of the base measures 0.002 metres, the width across the body is 0.01,8 metres and the loop-attachment is 0.005 metres long.

Plate VII 2

Found in the southern section of the main burial chamber were two banded agate beads and measuring 0.02,7 and 0.01,8 metres in length.

THE HIGHAM TUMULI

Graves 1, 5, 6, 7, 11, 23, 27, 30, 31, 32, 36, 37, 39, 40, 42, 44, 45, 46 Figs. 1, 3, 4a, c-e, 5-8, Plates VIII-XLII (Graves 33, 34, 38, 41, 43, 47(?) contained grave furnishings which are no longer in Captain Higham's possession).

Only 23 graves out of the 47 opened by Captain R. Higham R.S. contained burial gifts. This is most probably largely due to earlier grave robbery, since the excavator repeatedly refers to the fact that the graves had been entered at a time subsequent to interment, and most frequently via the east end of the mound.

Of the 23 tumuli containing grave objects, 13 graves belong to types 1-3 and can be marked as prehistoric (*Persica VI* 1972-1974). 10 graves belong to type 4 and must be dated to ca. 100 B.C.-100 A.D. (*Persica VI* 1972-1974).

6 of the earlier grave mounds had one alcove, only one grave had a total number of four and the other 6 graves had no alcove, being a simple rectangle. None of these 13 early tumuli had an upper storey. Their locations are scattered from south of the village of Sar to the southernmost moundfield on the west of the southern tip of the Jebal-ad-Dukhan (Fig. 1).

Higham Grave 1 — Moundfield South of Ain Umm Ijraiyi, East of Dumistan and North-East of Karzakkan (Location 2). Figs. 1, 4c, Plates VIII-IX.

This well and regularly built grave consisting of a main burial chamber without alcoves (see Tables I-II) contained one small-sized pyriform-shaped vessel with a pointed sagging base. It stood in an upright position placed on its base in the north-east corner of the burial chamber. This wheel-thrown vase has clearly visible rings on the inner surface. It has a slightly tapering neck with two fairly pronounced grooves and a thin, simple rim. Two fine and closely set shallowly engraved parallel lines encircle the upper shoulder just below the lowest groove. The clay which is well-tempered shows small white speckles or "exploding white grits" and is orangy/red with a purplish/red wash or paint which originally covered the entire outside of the vessel and extended partly into the inside. All that has remained of this paint or wash are small flaky patches. The height is 0.15 metres, the diameter of the rim measures 0.08,4 metres and the rim is 0.004 metres thick.

Higham Grave 5 — Moundfield South of Ain Umm Ijraiyi, East of Dumistan and North-East of Karzakkan (Location 2). Figs. 1, 5a, Plates X-XI, XIII 2.

This grave had no alcoves and positioned half way down its length and near to the northern wall, lay an oval-shaped pot. It was light brown to buff in colour, well-tempered and had a plain cylindrical, rimless neck of medium height, and the body tapered to a small, flattish, uneven base. A thin slip of the same, or possibly slightly darker colour, covers the entire surface to the base. Over this slip commencing at the junction of neck and shoulder, a purplish red wash or paint had been unevenly applied. This vessel appears to have been made by hand. That it was meant to hang rather than to stand upright, can be deduced by the fact that it bears on its shoulder and upper body the impression of a network of woven cloth, or woven or plaited reed. This had been tied to two horizontal and four vertical ropes, which have left wear marks on the body and the base where they were tied together. Moreover, the excavator comments that the pot lay on silted sand about 0.15 metres above the level of the skeleton. This could well indicate that the vessel had been suspended at the time of burial and had consequently fallen once the suspension had rotted. Such is the clarity of the marks that it can be observed that the knot under the base of the vessel was off-centre. At various places on the body and on the base the outer surface of the vessel has traces of blackening by burning. The height is 0.20 metres, the diameter of the rim measures 0.09,8-0.10 metres and the diameter of the base is 0.04,8 metres.

Higham Grave 31 — Moundfield South of Ain Sakhara and North-North-East of Dar Chulaib (Location 3). Figs. 1, 5 b, Plates XII-XIII 1-2.

A vase, comparable to the one from grave 5 (see above), lay just outside the alcove constructed at the east end of the northern wall of the main burial chamber. This vessel which lay on its side with the opening facing towards the east, is a light-brown to buff colour, fairly well levigated with white particles. It has an oval outline, is round-bellied, and has a high plain cylindrical neck with a simple slightly outturned thickened rim, and a small uneven flattish base. A thin slip of a slightly darker colour covers the entire vase and extends inside the rim. This slip originally bore a purplish-red paint or wash, which covered the entire outer surface including the neck, and possibly also its inside. The slip is flaking off badly, thus exposing the core of the vase and the purplish-red paint has also faded, but is still visible in faint patches. It seems likely that this vessel had also hung in ropes, the marks being visible at two points; one rope impression is seen running round the neck and a second one is visible just under the lowest point of the shoulder, at 0.05,5 metres from the flat base to be exact. It would seem that four or more vertical strings had been required to tie below the base, although the mark or imprint of one only, is now discernible. These would be attached to the horizontal ropes and thus cradle the pot in balance. The height is 0.16,1 metres, the diameter of the rim measures 0.09,6 metres and the diameter of the base is 0.06 metres.

Higham Grave 6 — Moundfield East of Malichiya and North-North-East of Ain Sakhara (Location 3a). Figs. 1, 4e, Plate XIV 1-2.

This tumulus had one alcove, which had been built at the east end of the northern wall of the main burial chamber. Within it a brick-red, well-tempered, pyriform vase with a medium high cylindrical ribbed neck and a roundish-pointed sagging base lay on its side, its base was turned towards, and lay at the same level as, the skull of the deceased which latter was sited in the main burial chamber of the grave. The upper part of the cylindrical neck of the base has 5 parallel very well defined ribbings, and the lower part is plain. The vase has a slightly darker red paint or wash, which has been applied over the brick-red clay of the vase, covering its entire outer surface as well as the upper part of the inside of the neck. A deep groove can be seen exteriorly, exactly at the junction of the neck and the shoulder which would seem to indicate that the neck was turned on to the body by means of a wheel. Augmenting this suggestion, is the presence of slight grooving on the inside of the neck, indicative of manufacture on the wheel. The body may have been made separately by hand and then joined, a supposition perhaps justified by the presence of an irregular, thickened ridge with finger marks, inside the neck at the precise junction with the shoulder. The height is 0.23,4 metres and the diameter of the rim measures 0.10,9-0.11 metres.

Higham Grave 7 — Moundfield South of Ain Sakhara and North-North-East of Dar Chulaib (Location 3). Figs. 1, 3b, 4d, 5c, Plates XV-XVIII.

The excavator remarks upon this grave that it was, "heavily silted, this making it difficult to observe the position of bones, badly defined mound in that it was partly below present ground level, and only about 5ft high." The structure consisted of one main burial chamber without alcoves, orientated east-west, and the funerary gifts accompanying the deceased were found at the western end.

Fig. 4d, Plates XV 1-2, XVIII 2.

There were three funerary vessels, the first described being in the most southerly position. It was a pyriform vase with a high cylindrical neck bearing eight deeply cut impressions covering the entire neck surface down to the almost horizontal junction of the shoulder. It has a roundish-pointed sagging base. The clay is brick red, with occasional white particles and is well-tempered, and the entire outer surface is covered with a reddish-purple paint or wash. It is comparable to the pyriform vase from grave 6 with a thickish ridge halfway down the inside of the cylindrical neck again indicating that the latter and the body had been fashioned separately, the neck being thrown on a wheel, the body modelled by hand, and that the two different parts had then been fitted together. The height is 0.18,5 metres, the diameter of the rim measures 0.09,3 metres and the width of the shoulder is 0.005-0.009 metres.

Fig. 5 c, Plates XVI 1-2, XVII 1, XVIII 2.

The central piece of the three funerary vessels was a shallow, open, rimless bowl with a fairly flat sagging base. It is made of a rather drab, light brown clay with possibly an irregularly applied pale yellow cast slip or wash. The texture is rather sandy and shows small white particles. This bowl is hand-made. An irregularly smeared, indeterminate purplish-reddish-brown paint, covers the inside and outside. The outside of the upper portion of the bowl bears two dark brown to black bands, the top one being broader than the lower one. These are barred eight separate times by groups of six to eight short vertical lines. A series of thumb or finger marks are visible just below the decoration. The unevenly shaped bowl bears on the inside, an irregular broad band of a purplish-brown paint. The height is 0.07,5 metres, the diameter of the rim measures 0.06,2-0.07,7 metres.

Fig. 3 b, Plates XVII 2, XVIII 1-2.

The most northerly situated of this group of three vessels is a deep, hand-made bowl on a small, and indistinctly indicated, flat base. It is made of a light brownish clay which had been tempered with coarse sand, white chalky bits, and pieces of chopped straw. The latter have left their impressions in the clay, inside as well as outside. The bowl has a light brown, sandy coloured wash. 2 to 3 centimetres below the outside rim are a series of thumb or finger impressions and the walls of the bowl have been pared inside and outside, the cutting marks being clearly visible. The height is 0.15 metres, the diameter of the rim measures 0.21,5-0.21,8 metres and the diameter of the base is 0.05,5-0.06 metres.

Higham Grave 11 — South-East of Moundfield South of Ain Sakhara and North-North-East of Dar Chulaib (Location 3). Fig. 1, Plate XIX 1.

Since this tomb lay partly below the present ground level, the excavator found it necessary to enter the chamber via the roof, On top of the sand filling the grave to within 0.23 metres of the roof, lay a typical ridged, rather badly flaked, but entire Barbar pot. The pot itself was apparently touching the roof. Unfortunately this vessel no longer belongs to the Higham collection, and although a photograph exists, it is insufficient to provide further detailed information. There was evidently a possibility of a previous entry to the tomb, and the exact position of the skeleton could not be determined as the bones were scattered. The skull lay at the east wall and leg bones at the western end.

Higham Grave 23 — Moundfield South-South-West of Sar and North-North-West of Buri (Location 5). Figs 1, 3 c, Plates XIX 2, XX 1.

In the alcove, which was built at the east end of the main burial chamber, lay a light-buff, finely grit-tempered vessel, showing in its texture innumerable small white speckles. It had an almost round body, a small flat base and a short neck, with an out-turned triangular rim. There is a very shallow groove at the junction of neck and shoulder, while just above it, near the end of the neck, a small number of irregularly spaced, short, incised lines are visible.

The neck and the upper part of the shoulder may have been thrown on a wheel, since rather widely spaced wheel rings are visible up to that point, whereas lower down the inner surface of the pot feels quite irregular and lumpy, suggesting that the lower portion of the body had been formed by hand. The walls have been pared. There are certain generic resemblances with the "Barbar" ware; the round body, the small flat base, the triangular rim and the brittle, gritty texture showing "white exploding grits", make it feasible to suggest a certain contemporaneity with the "Barbar" ware. The height is 0.21 metres, the diameter of the rim measures 0.10,7 metres and the diameter of the base is 0.07 metres.

Higham Grave 27 — Moundfield East of Wasmiya and West of Jebal-ad-Dukhan in the Neighbourhood of the Rim Rock (Location 4). Figs. 1, 3 d, Plate XX 2-3.

The grave was constructed without alcoves and halfway down the northern wall of the chamber, level with the pelvic bones of the deceased, lay a small handmade, sun-dried pot. Formed of drab grey clay, it has a round body and a flattish sagging base and the greater part of the neck and rim are missing. The remaining height is 0.09 metres, the diameter of the flattish base is ca. 0.02 metres and the walls are 0.005 metres in thickness.

Higham Grave 30 — Moundfield East of Malichiya and North-North-East of Ain Sakhara (Location 3 a). Fig. 1, Plate XXI 1.

The grave consisted only of a main burial chamber without alcoves and was filled with silt to a height within 0.60 metres of the capstones. On top of this lay a copper/bronze spearhead with a hollow socket. The total length of the remains of the weapon is 0.12,9 metres, the metal being 0.001 metres in thickness. The spearhead itself, measures 0.04 metres in length and 0.02 metres at its greatest width. Of its location on top of the silt, the excavator remarks that it" perhaps indicates that it was placed high in the wall and fell when shaft disintegrated."

Higham Grave 32 — Moundfield South of Ain Umm Ijraiyi, East of Dumistan and North-East of Karzakkan (Location 2). Figs. 1, 4a, Plates XXI 2, XXII 1-2.

A typical ridged, white speckled grit-tempered "Barbar" pot is reported to have lain in the alcove built at the eastern end of the north wall of the main burial chamber. The excavator also mentions "indication of small mat with traces of bitumen covering in alcove which disintegrated on touching." The pot is fairly large, has a round body with a short neck and an outturned triangular rim, and stands on a small flat base. The vessel sags considerably to one side and the low, flat base has collapsed under the weight of the pot as is clearly demonstrated by the compressed edges of the base. The height is 0.26 metres, the diameter of the rim is 0.15 metres and the diameter of the base measures 0.07,9 × 0.08,2 metres.

The pot appears to be wheel-thrown and the clay has a light brownish-red colour, the texture being brittle. A thin slip of the same colour as the clay itself covers the outer surface though in certain places this has turned yellowish-white. One portion of the pot has a scorched appearance which appears below the neck and continues down to the base. The surface has been worked up in low ridges, which have not been regularly drawn and which are wider spaced and better outlined on the upper portion of the shoulder than they are lower down. They are so shallowly raised that the core of the pot, though partly exposed, does not show any sign of their modelling. On the lower part of the vessel the ridges become mere incisions which in places overlap and appear crudely executed. The pot has two ancient holes, one roughly halfway down the body, the other just above the base. These had originally been plugged with bitumen, of which the remains were still present at the time of excavation. The repair indicates the value of the pot as a household object.

Higham Grave 46 — Moundfield East of Buri, South of Ali and North of the Hamala Road (Location 1). Fig. 1, Plates XXIII 1-4, XXIV 1.

One of a group of 5 large mounds contained an east-west orientated main burial chamber, furnished with 4 alcoves. Two of these were formed by extensions of the east wall, and thus faced one another across the head of the main chamber, and the other two followed a similar arrangement at the western end, so that the entire complex had an overall appearance of a shallow H-shape with the main chamber represented by the crosspiece.

Near the south wall of the main burial chamber, Captain Higham found an oval-shaped vessel with a cylindrical neck and a small flat base, reported to bear similarity to that from *Higham Grave* 5. Lying to the east side of this was the rim of a large vessel, stated to show signs of suspension cords. These two items are said to have been in Hannover, Germany, since 1971, and thus no further detailed comment can be elicited.

In the southernmost of the two alcoves extending from the west wall of the main chamber lay a number of beads, a pendant of mother-of-pearl in the shape of a bird, and various pieces of ivory which may have been inlays. These latter range in shape from thin, flat, almost square plaques to irregular shaped, rather rounded fragments. One narrow fragment has been engraved at one end with 4 close set, encircling parallel lines. Amongst these pieces Captain Higham mentions the possibility of broken ostrich shells.

The schematically rendered bird made of mother-of-pearl has a suspension hole perforating the up-turned wing. It measures 0.01,1 × 0.02,7 metres and has an overall thickness of 0.001-0.002 metres.

Of the 75 beads arbitrarily strung by Captain Higham, 6 pellet-like beads are made of agate, one oval-shaped bead is made of shell, one longish bead with an almost triangular cross-section is made from alabaster, and the remaining majority consisting largely of small pellet-like beads, appear to have been made of glass. Some have a mottled or veined blue colour, others are translucent, and yet others show a brownish coating with underneath it, a rather irregular bluish tinge. Although glass is known as dating from the third millennium B.C., the appearance of the glass beads in such numbers — 67 of the total of 75 — and the fact that some of the blue glass ones with white trails distinctly resemble Roman glass, would seem, in this case, to cast doubt on a third millennium B.C. dating. Additionally, Captain Higham reports "perhaps a secondary burial, one roof stone above smaller pot levered and wedged upwards at N side, perhaps to insert secondary burial." He also mentions "extensive traces of broken red pottery and some dark(black)." This grave was not fully explored, due to the imposition of a ban on illegal digging by the Bahrain Government. It is obviously difficult to substantiate from such meagre evidence, the suggested possibility of the presence of a secondary burial in this grave mound.

Higham Grave 36 — Mound South of the Portugese Fort and Near the Present Budaia—Manama Road (Location 6). Figs. 1, 6a-c, 7a, c-d, Plates I 3-4, II 1-4, XXIII, XXIV 2-5, XXV-XXXIII.

Grave 36 is the richest of 10 explored in one irregularly shaped mound roughly 4 metres high. The 10 graves, which were stone built and mud or cement-lined, have no noticeable preference for a specific orientation, and are reported to have been dug at five different levels of the mound. In *Persica VI* 1972-1974, p. 148, note 52* it was stated "Captain Higham numbered each of the 10 related graves investigated in this mound but in the absence of a comprehensive plan I have thought it better to use the richest grave (no. 36) as a focal point of reference in this paper. Original numbering will appear in Catalogue *Persica VII.*" The original numbering will, therefore, appear in this, the present Catalogue.

Grave 36 was mud-lined with bits of carbon embedded in the mud which covered the walls and the floor. The deceased was lying on his back with extended legs along the centre of the grave. The greater majority of the grave furnishings had been placed towards the feet of the body.

Fig. 7a, Plate XXXIII 1-3.

Left of the deceased in grave 36 at the lower end of the legs, stood a small round-bellied pot with a short, flat everted rim and a low ringbase, each of the same diameter. The body of the wheel-made pot is light buff in colour and a much weathered greenish-blue glaze with gold patches, coats the outside and extends as far down as possible inside the vessel. The height is 0.05,5 metres, the diameter of the rim measures 0.04,1 metres and the diameter of the base is also 0.04,1 metres.

Fig. 6a, Plates XXV 1-2, XXVI 1-2.

At the feet of the body in the left hand corner of the grave lay a deep purple milefiore pillar-moulded bowl with opaque white marbling. Twenty five ribs run below the straight neck to near the centre of the base which itself is slightly dimpled. A thick coating of blackish burned material covers the entire base and lower portion of this glass bowl. The height is 0.04,6 metres, the diameter of the rim measures 0.13 metres, the diameter of the concave base is ca. 0.04 metres and the height of the straight neck measures 0.01,5 metres. Its provenance could be either Alexandria, or even Italy, taking account of the excellent workmanship (see *Persica VI* 1972-1974, pp. 152-155).

Inside this pillar-moulded bowl lay a string of 38 agate, crystal and amethyst beads of varied shape, an ivory comb and a needle-shaped ivory pin which is now broken. In addition was a square piece of ivory with concave back, four crenelated corners and a concentric circle decoration. A copper spatula with a flat triangular head had been placed across the top of the glass bowl.

Plates XXIII 1, XXIX 2-3.

The beads have been re-strung by Captain Higham and consist of variously sized elongated, oval, or barrel-shaped beads with a roundish, an oval or a lentil-shaped cross-section. Further types include facetted, elongated and barrel-shaped beads, with roundish facetted cross-section. There are also truncated lozenge-shaped beads and a roundish pellet-shaped variety. The largest one, which is agate, measures 0.03,45 metres in length and the smallest measurements are those of pellet-like agate beads at 0.003 × 0.005 metres. One truncated lonzenge-shaped bead measures 0.006 × 0.004 metres and one roundish tiny amethyst bead is 0.006 × 0.005 metres.

Plate XXIV 3, 5.

The ivory comb which is in a very poor and broken condition measures 0.04 metres across by 0.03,1 metres in length and has an overall thickness of 0.001-0.002 metres.

Plate XXIV 4-5.

The square ivory plaque with its concave back is also in a broken condition and measures 0.03,8 × 0.03,8 metres taken across the slightly embossed front. Two deeply carved circles form part of the design, the outer one of which takes up the entire diameter of the piece and isolates the four crenelated corners. The thickness of this decorative ivory piece is 0.002 metres.

Plate XXIV 2.

The fragmentary ivory needle-shaped pin, which is broken in two pieces, one measuring 0.07 metres and the other fragment 0.08 metres, has an encircling incision on the thicker broken end. The diameter at the two ends is 0.005-0.006 metres and 0.003 metres or even less.

Plates XXIV 5, XXX 4.

The copper/bronze spatula, which had been placed across the top of the glass bowl has not yet been cleaned. As far as can be ascertained in its corroded state, it appears to be circular in cross-section with a slight thickening towards its end. The total length of this spatula is 0.15,4 metres, the width of the flat triangular head, measured at its extremity, measures 0.01,1 metres. The cross-section at the transsition of the flat head and the round stem measures 0.002,5 metres whereas the cross-section towards the other circular end is 0.003,5 metres.

Next to the pillar-moulded bowl lay a closely arranged group of 4 vessels. They were aligned alongside the short wall, directly at the feet of the deceased. Left to right as seen from above the grave the first to be considered is a milky white glass cup next to the pillar-moulded bowl and adjacent to the feet. Behind this lay a blue amphorisk, followed by a glazed pilgrim flask and finally a greenish-white glass vessel described by the excavator as "similar to the blue vase."

Fig. 6c, Plates XXVII 1-2, XXVIII 1-2.

The milky white, non-translucent and rimless cup mentioned first above, has a globular body and a flattish, sagging base. As in the case of the pillar-moulded bowl, it has a thick coating of burnt material, a small amount of which is adherent to the base, and the remainder to the side of the vessel, suggesting that it was in a reclining position during at least a part of the burning process. The cup is of a shape common in the mid 1st century A.D., and its most likely area of manufacture would be the workshops of Syria where a preference for white glass was current. However, this shape was commonly created in translucent glass, and equipped with a painted lid. White glass was used for other shapes, and was also incorporated with other colourings, but a non-translucent cup such as that under discussion is very unique. The height is 0.06,3-0.06,6 metres and the diameter of the rim measures 0.07,9-0.08,2 metres.

Fig. 6b, Plate XXIX 1.

Close to the milky white cup but slightly to the rear lay the small milefiore amphorisk of blue glass, ornamented with whitish trails. It is suggested that this vessel should be dated to the middle of the first century A.D. (see *Persica VI* 1972-1974, pp. 152-155). The height is 0.12 metres, the diameter of the rim 0.01,8-0.02 metres and the rim itself has a thickness of 0.002-0.003,5 metres.

Fig. 7c-d, Plates XXXI 1-2, XXXII 1, XXIII 3.

Of the two remaining vessels, which stood at the feet of the deceased the next one was a well-preserved pilgrim flask with a bluish-green glaze with gold undertones. The shape is bulbous front and back, and typically separated by a concave continuous band from which rise lug handles placed at either side of the neck. The handles are somewhat pointed on the upper outline and are perforated by small holes. On the outer aspect the thick walled cylindrical neck is created with two grooves, the flange between them protruding sharply. The inner side of the rim curves down to the actual mouth opening. The height is 0.11 metres, the total thickness of the bulbous body at its widest point is 0.05,5 metres, and the concave sides included therein, have a width of 0.02,6-0.02,7 metres. The height of the pierced lugs is 0.02,5 metres, their width is 0.01,8-0.02 metres and the diameter of the perforations is 0.006-0.007 metres. The actual throat of the flask measures 0.008 metres.

Unfortunately, Captain Higham reports that the last of the assemblage of four vessels no longer belongs to his collection. It was found at the right hand corner of the foot of the grave and although he describes it as "similar to the blue vase," referring to the small blue amphorisk, his hasty sketch gives no indication of handles and the lower part of the body is missing. The vessel is reputed to have been of a pale green and white glass and to have incorporated "inlaid wire spirals", twice obliquely encircling the neck and twice crossing the remains of the pear-shaped body. The querry was posed as to whether the metal may have been silver, which having oxydised, resulted in darkened outlines. The measurements divulged by Higham are approximately 0.08,2 metres across the body and 0.06,3 metres for the length of the neck which is drawn as having a small everted rim.

Plates XXX 3, XL 4.

In the approximate position of the left knee of the deceased lay a double-pronged iron hook, the shaft of one side being broken. Its use as a means of attachment for a dagger to a belt has been conjectured (*Persica VI* 1972-1974, pp. 150, 152). The measurements of this very corroded piece of iron can be only an approximation. The total length of the complete prong is about 0.06,35 metres and the width of the connecting structure is ca. 0.01,5 metres.

Plate XXX 1-2.

Above the prong and near the left side of the pelvis of the skeleton lay three dome-shaped or conical pinheads of ivory and steatite with the remains of thin copper and iron rods still sited in their central perforations. The head of one of these copper rods is decorated with two parallel ridges and a series of tiny, empty circles, apparently meant to take a kind of inlay. Out of the total number of a dozen pinheads coming from these 10 graves, one only was made of silver. Their height varies from 0.004 to 0.008 metres, the diameter at their base from 0.01,1 to 0.01,6 metres.

The excavator, however, was not entirely specific about the circumstances and findsports of each separate pinhead discovered in the complex of 10 cement- or mud-lined graves entered by him, in this one irregularly shaped mound. It has, therefore, been thought better illustrate the pinheads from the different graves together in one Plate rather than to attempt to fit them into the various groups of grave furnishings and thus risk classifying them upon insufficient and sometimes vague information. Near the neck of the deceased at the same side as the iron hook and the three pinheads Captain Higham discovered two plain gold earrings. Their present whereabouts cannot be ascertained, as they are no longer in his possession and unfortunately a detailed description is unavailable.

Higham Grave 37 — Mound South of the Portugese Fort and Near the Present Budaia — Manama Road (Location 6). Figs. 1, 8 d, Plates I 4-5, II 1-4, XXXIV 1-3, XLI 1.

Grave 37 was ca. 1.22 metres below grave 36, and about 1.52 metres to the south. The deceased was lying on the right side in an attitude of flexion with the spine against the long wall and the head ca. 0.71 metres from the short-sided head wall.

The position of the three objects which were reported by the excavator is not clearly stated and only one of them still belongs to his collection. This latter is a small wheelmade, greenish-blue glazed vase. It is pear-shaped, with a tapering neck terminating in a small everted rim, a low concave ringbase, and originally one handle of which only the stubs remain. The much weathered glaze is underlaid by large portions of a gold tinge and covers the entire outer surface as well as extending down the sloping everted neck rim as far as the narrowest point of the throat of the vessel. The height is 0.10,3-0.10,8 metres, the diameter of the rim measures 0.02,8 metres and the diameter of the hollow ringbase is 0.04,5 metres. The other two objects in grave 37 are no longer part of Captain Higham's collection but have been described briefly, by him, as follows. "The base of a larger vessel, and a broken spatula, tested by dissolving oxide in H CL and was found to be rolled copper plate flattened at one end." It is mentioned that it was similar to the one discovered lying across the pillar-moulded glass bowl in grave 36, as already been recorded above.

Higham Grave 38 was on the same level as 37 but situated ca. 2.44 metres to the south. It was mud-lined with rounded corners and had bits of charcoal embedded in the floor and walls. The deceased was positioned along the axis of the grave on his back and with extended legs. The head was nearly touching the head wall. A glazed grave pot is reported to be in the U.S.A. but was small, round-bodied with a short, flat everted rim and a low-hollow ringbase similar to that described in grave 36 and presumably wheelmade. It stood on its base at the right hand side of the body near the pelvis.

Higham Grave 39 — Mound South of the Portugese Fort and near the Present Budaia—Manama Road (Location 6). Figs. 1, 8a, Plates I 4-5, II 1-4, XXXV 1-2, XXXIX 1-2.

Grave 39 was the third grave of the same depth as grave 36. It was dug 3.66 metres to the south of grave 37. The deceased had been placed in the north-west corner of the grave lying on his right side and in the south-west corner a wheelmade round-bodied pot with a short neck with a flat everted rim and a low hollow ringbase was discovered. It bears a bluish-green glaze, with an undertone of yellowish-gold which covers the whole pot, including the base, the rim and the inside of the latter. The height is 0.17,5 metres, the diameter of the rim measures 0.09,6-0.09,7 metres and the diameter of the ringbase is 0.07,2 metres.

Higham Grave 40 — Mound South of the Portugese Fort and near the Present Budaia—Manama Road (Location 6). Figs. 1, 8 c, Plates I 4-5, II 1-4, XXX 1-2, XXXVI 1-2, XXXIX 1-2.

Ca. 1.83 metres to the north of grave 37 at the same level as the latter and therefore found on a level ca. 1.22 metres beneath grave 36, is grave 40. The deceased had been placed on his right side, along the northern wall with the head ca. 0.30 metres from the western wall, and had been furnished with a wheelmade, glazed, round-bodied jar with a fairly high neck and a flat everted rim, a low concave ringbase and two small lug-like handles between rim and shoulder. A greenish glaze with an undertone of yellowish-gold covers the entire outer surface, including the base and the inside of the rim. This vessel which had been placed in the centre of the southern wall measures 0.19,4 metres high. The diameter of the rim is 0.08 metres and that of the concave ringbase 0.07,9 metres. Two pinheads lay near the pelvis of the body.

Higham Grave 42 — Mound South of the Portugese Fort and near the Present Budaia—Manama Road (Location 6). Figs. 1, 7 b, Plates I 4-5, II 1-4, XXX 2-3, XXXVII 1-2, XXXVIII 1, XXXIX 1-2, XL 1-2,4.

Grave 42 was dug to the same depth as grave 36 and was positioned 5.49 metres north-west of grave 36. The deceased rested on his back with extended legs along the axis of the grave, with the head 0.15 metres from the north-west wall and the right arm placed across the body. On one of the fingers of the left hand, and still in situ, was a much corroded and broken copper finger-ring. It was built up of two separate plain bands of which only one was complete. Fixed on to these is a medallion-like central piece which appears to have remained undecorated. The diameter of the two parallel copper rings is ca. 0.02 metres, the width of the circular central piece is ca. 0.01 metres. The overall thickness of the copper is 0.003-0.005 metres. Fragments of a plain bronze/(?)bangle, which since the pieces do not fit, may represent more than one item, were found at the right side of the chest. With them was a complete bangle in which the two extremities overlap alongside each other. The diameter of the complete bangle measures 0.04,5 metres and the thickness of the metal of both bangles varies from 0.003-0.004 metres. Five agate beads lay on the left side of the body 0.10 metres away from the previously mentioned finger-ring. A double-pronged hook about 0.05 metres long was found above the right shoulder of the body and can be compared with a similar iron hook which was found near the knees of the body in grave 36.

A wheelmade bluish-green glazed jar with a round body, a short, fairly wide neck with an everted rim and a low concave ringbase, was also discovered. The glaze which has an undertone of yellowish-gold, covers the entire outside surface, including the low ringbase, but does not seem to have extended inside the rim. Two small pierced lugs are placed at the junction of shoulder and neck. A series of low, vertical incisions cover the upper part of the body extending down to the maximum diameter. The height varies between 0.12,7-0.13,7 metres due to the fact that the pot does not stand straight, the diameter of the rim measures 0.06,3 metres and the diameter of the base is 0.05,7 metres. The low, vertical incisions are 0.005-0.01,2 metres apart and each is 0.03-0.03,5 metres long.

Higham Grave 43 which was at a slightly higher level than no. 40 is reported to have small dimensions with rounded corners and to be built only of mud, which had carbon remains in the walls and the floor. A goldish-coloured glazed open bowl on a high base was discovered in this grave and is thought to be in Bahrain. The height is reported to be 0.20,3 metres and the diameter of the rim is given as ca. 0.35,5 metres. Regrettably again further information is lacking.

Higham Grave 44 — Mound South of the Portugese Fort and near the Present Budaia — Manama Road (Location 6). Figs. 1, 8 e, Plates XLI 1-3.

Grave 44 was dug to about the same level as grave 37 and lay between graves 36, 40 and 42, although 1.52 metres lower down. The deceased lay on his left side with extended legs along the west wall of the grave with the head 0.20 metres from the northern wall. A small wheelmade high-necked jar with an everted rim, a low, concave base and two high-swung handles had been placed at the knees of the body 0.08 metres away from the east wall. A greenish-blue glaze with a strong yellow-gold undertone, which has partly disappeared, covered the entire outside of the jar. The pear-shaped body shows a fairly sharp carination at the lower part of the body and the whole vessel sags decidedly to one side. The height is 0.10,8 metres, the diameter of the rim measures 0.02,8 metres and the diameter of the base is 0.04,2 metres. The diameter of the actual mouth opening inside the gently down-sloped neck is 0.005 metres. The handles are 0.03,6 metres high.

Higham Grave 45 — Mound South of the Portugese Fort and near the Present Budaia — Manama Road (Location 6). Figs. 1, 8 b, Plates XXXIII 3, XLII 1-3.

Grave 45 was situated on the western extremity of the same irregularly shaped mound, ca. 4.57 metres to the west of grave 36 at a ca. 1.22 metres lower level.

At the feet of the deceased who lay on his back with his arms clasped at the abdomen in the centre of the grave, lay a wheelmade whitish glazed, shallow, rimless bowl on a very slightly hollowed small base. The glaze covers the entire inner and outer surface, including the base. A bluish colour is only visible on the inside of the rim. The height is 0.05,3 metres, the diameter of the rim measures 0.15,2 metres and the diameter of the base is 0.05,2 metres.

TABLE I

Architectural Features of the Graves, Location of the Body

	JEFFERSON GRAVE	HIGHAM GRAVE 1	HIGHAM GRAVE 2	HIGHAM GRAVE 3
grave location	Hamala North see map	location 2 see map	location 2 see map	location 2 see map
textual references	see pp. 3-6, 42-44, 45	see pp. 7, 42, 45	——	——
measurements tumulus	ht. c. 3,05 m. dm. foot c. 16,75 m.	ht. 2,49 m. dm. foot 4,57 m.	ht. 1,98 m. dm. foot 3,66 m.	ht. 2,29 m. dm. foot 4,27 m.
measurements burial chamber	l. 2,74 m. w. c. 0,71 m. ht. 0,99-1,08 m.	l. 2,54 m. w. 0,94 m. ht. 1,52 m.	l. 2,18 m. w. 1,02 m. ht. 1,27 m.	l. 2,13 m. w. 0,86 m. ht. 1,24 m.
presence alcoves	2 at east end of burial chamber	——	——	——
measurements alcoves	east end north wall l. c. 0,61 m.; w. c. 0,61 m.; ht. 0,76-0,84 m. east end south wall l. c. 0,91 m.; w. c. 0,61 m.; ht. 0,76-0,84 m.	——	——	——
number capstones a) chamber b) alcoves	a) 4 b) 1	a) 4	a) 4	a) 5
orientation burial chamber	east-west entrance facing west	east-west	east-west	east-west
orientation body	east-west	east-west	east-west	east-west
location body	head near east wall feet facing western entrance	head near east wall feet facing western entrance	head in south-east corner leg bones pointing towards north-west corner	bones along south wall
attitude body	extended position	attitude of flexion	sitting position with extended legs(?)	extended position
remarks		core of mound built up of coarse stones, outer layers of smaller stones and sand	core of mound built up of coarse stones, outer layers of smaller stones and sand	some large, non-human bones in north-eastern corner of main burial chamber core of mound built up of coarse stones, outer layers of smaller stones and sand

HIGHAM GRAVE 4	HIGHAM GRAVE 5	HIGHAM GRAVE 6	HIGHAM GRAVE 7	HIGHAM GRAVE 8
location 2 see map	location 2 see map	location 3a see map	location 3 see map	location 3 see map
——	see pp. 7-8, 42, 46	see pp. 42, 46	see pp. 9-10, 42, 45	——
ht. 2,44 m. dm. foot 3,66 m.	ht. 2,13 m. dm. foot 3,35 m.	ht. 2,44 m. dm. foot 3,96 m.	ht. c. 1,52 m. dm. foot 3,50.5 m.	ht. 1,29.5 m. dm. foot 3,20 m.
l. 2,03 m. w. 0,84 m. ht. 1,27 m.	l. 1,73 m. w. 0,74 m. ht. 1,24 m.	l. 1,93 m. w. 0,81 m. ht. 1,17 m.	l. 1,78 m. w. 0,89 m. ht. 1,50 m.	l. 1,78 m. w. 0,86 m. ht. 1,22 m.
——	——	1 at east end of northern wall	——	——
——	——	l. 0,41 m. w. 0,43 m. ht. 0,35.5 m.	——	——
a) 3	a) 3	a) 4 b) 1(?)	a) 3	a) 3
east-west	east-west	east-west	east-west	east-west
east-west	east-west	east-west	east-west	east-west
head in centre of chamber spine curved towards centre of chamber other bones nearer to west end	body along south wall facing north head 0,61 m. from east wall	body along south wall near centre of tomb head 0,23 m. from east wall	body along south wall head 0,30 m. from east wall	few fragments of bone throughout grave remains of skull at east end 0,25 m. from east wall
attitude of flexion	attitude of flexion	attitude of flexion	attitude of flexion(?)	undetermined
core of mound built up of coarse stones, outer layers of smaller stones and sand	core of mound built up of coarse stones, outer layers of smaller stones and sand			floor of grave ca. 0,46 m. below present ground level

	HIGHAM GRAVE 9	HIGHAM GRAVE 10	HIGHAM GRAVE 11	HIGHAM GRAVE 12(a)
grave location	location 3 see map	location 3 see map	location south-east of 3 see map	location 3a see map
textual references	——	——	see pp. 10, 42	——
measurements tumulus	ht. 1,68 m. dm. foot 3,05 m.	ht. 1,83 m. dm. foot 3,50.5 m.	——	——
measurements burial chamber	l. 1,78 m. w. 0,91 m. ht. 1,07 m.	l. 1,73 m. w. 0,79 m. ht. 1,09 m.	l. 1,60 m. w. 0,86 m. ht. 1,22 m.	l. 1,78 m. w. 0,96.5 m. ht. 1,17 m.
presence alcoves	1 at east end of northern wall	——	——	——
measurements alcoves	l. 0,23 m. w. 0,30 m. ht. 1,07 m.	——	——	——
number capstones a) chamber b) alcoves	a) 4 b) 1(?)	a) 4	a) 4	a) 3
orientation burial chamber	east-west	east-west	east-west	east-west
orientation body	east-west	east-west	east-west	probably east-west
location body	traces of bone throughout grave	traces of bone throughout grave	scattered bones head near east wall leg bones at west end	few traces of bone
attitude body	undetermined	undetermined	undetermined	undetermined
remarks	grave no. 9 was located between nos. 8 and 7 and was partly (ca. 0,30 m.) below present ground level	very roughly constructed grave with walls tapering towards a roof width of 0,56 m.		eastern extremity of location 3a

HIGHAM GRAVE 12(b)	HIGHAM GRAVE 13	HIGHAM GRAVE 14	HIGHAM GRAVE 15	HIGHAM GRAVE 16
location 2a see map	location 3 see map	location 3 see map	location 3 see map	location 5 see map
——	——	——	——	——
ht. 0.91,4 m. dm. foot 3,35 m.	——	——	——	ht. 3,05 m. dm. foot 5,18 m.
l. 1,93 m. w. 0,91 m. ht. 1,27 m.	dm. 1,17 m. ht. 0,86 m.	dm. 1,22 m. ht. 0,91 m.	dm. 1,12 m. ht. 0,86 m.	l. 2,21 m. w. 0,91 m. ht. 1,37 m.
——	——	——	——	1 at east end of northern wall
——	——	——	——	l. 0,41 m. w. 0,33 m. ht. 1,37 m.
a) 4	—— (not recorded)	—— (not recorded)	—— (not recorded)	a) 3 b) 1(?)
east-west	—— (not recorded)	—— (not recorded)	—— (not recorded)	east-west
east-west	undetermined	undetermined	undetermined	east-west
few bones along south wall	traces of bone throughout grave	traces of bone throughout grave	traces of bone throughout grave	body along south wall head 0,46 m. from east wall
undetermined	undetermined	undetermined	undetermined	on the back with extended legs
	southern extremity of location 3	southern extremity of location 3 traces of red pottery		

	HIGHAM GRAVE 17	HIGHAM GRAVE 18	HIGHAM GRAVE 19	HIGHAM GRAVE 20
grave location	location 5 see map	location 5 see map	location 5 see map	location 5 see map
textual references	———	———	———	———
measurements tumulus	ht. 2,44 m. dm. foot 3,96 m.	ht. 2,44 m. dm. foot 4,42 m.	ht. 2,44 m. dm. foot 4,11 m.	ht. 2,44 m. dm. foot 4,27 m.
measurements burial chamber	l. 2,13 m. w. 0,84 m. ht. 1,19 m.	l. 2,54 m. w. 0,94 m. ht. 1,47 m.	l. 2,62 m. w. 0,94 m. ht. 1,22 m.	l. 2,16 m. w. 0,86 m. ht. 1,22 m.
presence alcoves	———	1 at east end of northern wall	1 at east end of northern wall	2 at east end of burial chamber
measurements alcoves	———	l. 0,51 m. w. 0,41 m. ht. 0,51 m.	l. 0,51 m. w. 0,33 m. ht. 0,61 m.	east end north wall l. 0,51 m.; w. 0,30 m.; ht. 0,46 m. east end south wall l. 0,48 m.; w. 0,30 m.; ht. 0.56 m.
number capstones a) chamber b) alcoves	a) 4	a) 4 b) 1(?)	a) 4 b) 1(?)	a) 4 b) 1(?)+ 1(?)
orientation burial chamber	east-west	east-west	east-west	east-west
orientation body	east-west	east-west	undetermined	east-west
location body	body along north wall	body along south wall	traces of bone	fragments of bone along south wall head 0,38 m. from east wall
attitude body	on the back with extended legs	attitude of flexion on right side	undetermined	undetermined
remarks				

HIGHAM GRAVE 21	HIGHAM GRAVE 22	HIGHAM GRAVE 23	HIGHAM GRAVE 24	HIGHAM GRAVE 25
location 5 see map	location 5 see map	location 5 see map	location 1 see map	location 1 see map
——	——	see pp. 42, 44	——	——
ht. 2,51 m. dm. foot 4,11 m.	ht. 2,29 m. dm. foot 3,96 m.	ht. 2,44 m. dm. foot 3,35 m.	——	ht. 1,83 m. dm. foot 3,96 m.
l. 2,08 m. w. 0,86 m. ht. 1,29.5 m.	l. 2,01 m. w. 0,86 m. ht. 1,27 m.	l. 2,11 m. w. 0,86 m. ht. 1,24 m.	l. 1,83 m. w. 0,84 m. ht. 1,17 m.	l. 1,93 m. w. 0,81 m. ht. 1,12 m.
——	——	1 at east end of northern wall	——	——
——	——	l. 0,51 m. w. 0,35.5 m. ht. 0,61 m.	——	——
a) 4	a) 4	a) 4 b) 1(?)	a) 3	a) 2
east-west	east-west	east-west	east-west	east-west
east-west	east-west	east-west	undetermined	undetermined
not recorded	not recorded	body along south wall head 0,30 m. from east wall	no traces left	no traces left
on the back with extended legs(?)	on the back with extended legs	attitude of flexion on right side	undetermined	undetermined
very roughly constructed grave with walls tapering towards a roof width of 0,61 m.			very roughly constructed grave, partly beneath present ground level	

	HIGHAM GRAVE 26	HIGHAM GRAVE 27	HIGHAM GRAVE 28	HIGHAM GRAVE 29
grave location	location 1 see map	location 4 see map	location 4 see map	location 4 see map
textual references	——	see pp. 11, 42, 44	——	——
measurements tumulus	ht. 1,52 m. dm. foot 3,66 m.	ht. 2,74 m. dm. foot 4,88 m.	ht. 2,29 m. dm. foot 3,81 m.	ht. 2,44 m. dm. foot 3,96 m.
measurements burial chamber	l. 1,83 m. w. 0,89 m. ht. 1,24 m.	l. 3,25 m. w. 1,02 m. ht. 1,47 m.	l. 1,85 m. w. 0,81 m. ht. 1,35 m.	l. 2,13 m. w. 0,86 m. ht. 1,35 m.
presence alcoves	2 at east end of burial chamber	——	1 at east end of northern wall	——
measurements alcoves	east end north wall l. 0,35.5 m.; w. 0,23 m.; ht. 0,30 m. east and south wall l. 0,30 m.; w. 0,30 m.; ht. 0,35.5 m.	——	l. 0,38 m. w. 0,23 m. ht. 0,61 m.	——
number capstones a) chamber b) alcoves	a) 2 b) 1(?)+1(?)	a) 4	a) 2 b) 1(?)	a) 3
orientation burial chamber	east-west	east-west	east-west	east-west
orientation body	undetermined	east-west	east-west	undetermined
location body	no traces left	body along south wall	body in middle of grave head 0,25 m. from east wall	undetermined
attitude body	undetermined	attitude of flexion	on the stomach with extended legs(?)	undetermined
remarks		walls of burial chamber taper towards a roof width of 0,68.5 m.		

HIGHAM GRAVE 30	HIGHAM GRAVE 31	HIGHAM GRAVE 32	HIGHAM GRAVE 33	HIGHAM GRAVE 34
location 3a see map	location 3 see map	location 2 see map	location 3 see map	location 3 see map
see pp. 11, 42	see pp. 8, 42, 44	see pp. 12, 45	——	——
——	ht. 2,44 m. dm. foot 3,96 m.	——	——	——
l. 1,90.5 m. w. 0,91 m. ht. 1,17 m.	l. 1,80 m. w. 0,81 m. ht. 1,17 m.	l. 2,13 m. w. 0,94 m. ht. 1,40 m.	l. 1,93 m. w. 0,91 m. ht. 1,47 m.	l. 2,03 m. w. 0,91 m. ht. 1,32 m.
——	1 at east end of northern wall	1 at east end of northern wall	1 at east end of northern wall	1 at east end of northern wall
——	l. 0,41 m. w. 0,33 m. ht. 0,61 m.	l. 0,56 m. w. 0,43 m. ht. 0,61 m.	l. 0,41 m. w. 0,43 m. ht. 0,61 m.	l. 0,56 m. w. 0,46 m. ht. 0,63.5 m.
a) 4	a) 3	a) 3 b) 1(?)	a) 4 b) 1(?)	a) 4 b) 1(?)
east-west	east-west	east-west	east-west	east-west
undetermined	east-west	east-west	east-west	east-west
undetermined	body along south wall head 0,15 m. from east wall	body along south wall head 0,38 m. from east wall	body along south wall	body along south wall head 0,20 m. from east wall
undetermined	attitude of flexion on right side	attitude of flexion on right side	attitude of flexion	attitude of flexion

	HIGHAM GRAVE 35	HIGHAM GRAVE 36	HIGHAM GRAVE 37	HIGHAM GRAVE 38
grave location	location 2 see map	location 6 see map	location 6 see map	location 6 see map
textual references	——	see pp. 13-17, 42, 47-48	see pp. 18, 42, 49	see pp. 18, 42
measurements tumulus	ht. 2,59 m. dm. foot 4,11 m.	——	——	——
measurements burial chamber	l. 2,01 m. w. 0,91 m. ht. 1,32 m.	l. 2,46 m. w. 1,02 m. ht. 1,22 m.	l. 2,46 m. w. 0,89 m. ht. 1,24 m.	l. 1,98 m. w. 0,86 m. ht. 1,19 m.
presence alcoves	——	——	——	——
measurements alcoves	——	——	——	——
number capstones a) chamber b) alcoves	a) 4	—— (not recorded)	—— (not recorded)	—— (not recorded)
orientation burial chamber	east-west	70° from north	40° from north	120° from north
orientation body	undetermined	not recorded	not recorded	not recorded
location body	undetermined	body along centre of grave	head 0,71 m. from head wall spine against side wall	body along centre of grave head 0,06 m. from head wall
attitude body	undetermined	on the back with extended legs	attitude of flexion on right side	on the back with extended legs
remarks		grave is mud-lined with carbon embedded in mud covering walls and floor		grave has rounded corners with traces of carbon embedded in floor and walls

HIGHAM GRAVE 39	HIGHAM GRAVE 40	HIGHAM GRAVE 41	HIGHAM GRAVE 42	HIGHAM GRAVE 43
location 6 see map	location 6 see map	location 6 see map	location 6 see map	location 6 see map
see pp. 18-19, 42, 49	see pp. 19, 42, 49	———	see pp. 19-20, 42, 48	see pp. 20, 42, 48
———	———	———	———	———
l. 2,44 m. w. 0,94 m. ht. 1,17 m.	l. 2,44 m. w. 0,86 m. ht. 1,17 m.	l. 2,21 m. w. 0,84 m. ht. 1,02 m.	l. 2,44 m. w. 0,96.5 m. ht. 1,02 m.	l. 0,76 m. w. 0,41 m. ht. 0,38 m.
———	———	———	———	———
———	———	———	———	———
——— (not recorded)	——— (not recorded)	——— (not recorded)	——— (not recorded)	——— (not recorded)
80° from north	140° from north	80° from north	140° from north	90° from north
not recorded	not recorded	not recorded	not recorded	not recorded
body in north-west corner	body along north wall head 0,30 m. from west wall	body along north wall head 0,15 m. from west wall	body along axis of grave head 0,15 m. from north-west wall	traces of bone
attitude of flexion on right side	on right side attitude of flexion (?) (not recorded)	on the back with extended legs	on the back with extended legs right arm across body	undetermined
		location in the mound between graves 40 and 36, ca. 2,13 m. below grave 40		

	HIGHAM GRAVE 44	HIGHAM GRAVE 45	HIGHAM GRAVE 46	HIGHAM GRAVE 47
grave location	location 6 see map	location 6 see map	location 1 see map	location 1 see map
textual references	see pp. 20, 42, 49	see pp. 20-21, 42, 49	see pp. 12-13, 42	——
measurements tumulus	——	——	——	——
measurements burial chamber	l. 1,95.5 m. w. 0,81 m. ht. 0,81 m.	l. 2,21 m. w. 0,94 m. ht. 0,91 m.	l. 5,49 m. w. 1,29.5 m. ht. 1,47 m.	l. 5,49 m. w. 1,22 m. ht. 1,37 m.
presence alcoves	——	——	2 at east end and 2 at west end of burial chamber	2 at east end and 2 at west end of burial chamber
measurements alcoves	——	——	2 at east end l. 2,30 m.; w. 1,22 m.; ht. 1,47 m. 2 at west end l. ?; w. 1,22 m.; ht. 1,45 m.	2 at east end l. c. 2,44 m.; other measurements of the 4 alcoves not recorded
number capstones a) chamber b) alcoves	—— (not recorded)	—— (not recorded)	a) not recorded b) not recorded	a) not recorded b) not recorded
orientation burial chamber	20° from north	70° from north	east-west	east-west
orientation body	not recorded	not recorded	undetermined	not recorded
location body	body along west wall head 0,20 m. from north wall	body in centre along axis of grave head 0,25 m. from north-east wall	undetermined	not recorded
attitude body	on left side with extended legs	on the back with arms clasped(?) at abdomen	undetermined	not recorded
remarks	small grave with rounded corners, only of mud with carbon embedded in floor and walls			

TABLE II

The Funerary Gifts

TABLE II

	JEFFERSON GRAVE	HIGHAM GRAVE 1	HIGHAM GRAVE 5	HIGHAM GRAVE 6
pottery a) decorated b) plain c) glazed	a) X(1) b) X(1-4)	b) X(1)	b) X(1)	b) X(1)
location in grave	a) 1) against south wall b) 1) against south wall 2) against south wall 3) against west wall 4) against west wall	b) 1) north-east corner of burial chamber	b) 1) near north wall of burial chamber	b) 1) inside alcove at east end of north wall of burial chamber
glass ware				
location in grave				
utilitarian metal objects	X(1-3)			
location in grave	1) left of skull and against north wall 2) against north wall 3) against north wall			
ivory objects				
location in grave				
decorative pieces a) metal b) ivory c) semi-precious stone d) varia	a) X(1) c) X(1-2)			
location in grave	a) 1) northern section of burial chamber c) 1-2) southern section of burial chamber			
pinheads				
location in grave				
remarks				

HIGHAM GRAVE 7	HIGHAM GRAVE 11	HIGHAM GRAVE 23	HIGHAM GRAVE 27	HIGHAM GRAVE 30
a) X(1) b) X(1-2)	b) X(1)	b) X(1)	b) X(1)	
a) 1) west end of burial chamber b) 1) west end of burial chamber 2) west end of burial chamber	b) 1) on top of sand filling burial chamber	b) 1) inside alcove at east end of north wall of burial chamber	b) 1) against north wall of burial chamber	
				X(1)
				1) on top of silt within 0,60 m. of capstones

TABLE II

	HIGHAM GRAVE 31	HIGHAM GRAVE 32	HIGHAM GRAVE 33	HIGHAM GRAVE 34
pottery a) decorated b) plain c) glazed	b) X(1)	b) X(1)	b) X(1)	b) X(1-2)
location in grave	b) 1) just outside alcove at east end of north wall of burial chamber	b) 1) inside alcove at east end of north wall of burial chamber	b) 1) inside alcove at east end of north wall of burial chamber similar to grave 31 does not belong to this collection	b) 1-2) inside alcove at east end of north wall of burial chamber(?) similar to grave 23(?) does not belong to this collection
glass ware				
location in grave				
utilitarian metal objects				
location in grave				
ivory objects				
location in grave				
decorative pieces a) metal b) ivory c) semi-precious stone d) varia				
location in grave				
pinheads				
location in grave				
remarks	two non-human bones in alcove	small bones in alcove; "indication of small mat with traces of bitumen covering in alcove, which disintegrated on touching."	bones of goat and sheep at west end of grave; skull of deceased mediterranean type (Am. Mus. Nat. Hist. N.Y.)	

HIGHAM GRAVE 36	HIGHAM GRAVE 37	HIGHAM GRAVE 38	HIGHAM GRAVE 39	HIGHAM GRAVE 40
c) X(1-2)	c) X(1-2)	c) X(1)	c) X(1)	c) X(1)
c) 1) lower left end of legs of body 2) at feet of body	c) 1) not recorded 2) not recorded does not belong to this collection (p. 18)	c) 1) right of body near pelvis similar to grave 36 does not belong to this collection (p. 18)	c) 1) south-west corner of grave	c) 1) in centre of south wall
X(1-4)				
1) at feet of body 2) at feet of body 3) at feet of body 4) at feet of body does not belong to this collection (pp. 16-17)				
X(1-2)	X(1)			
1) placed across top of glass bowl (see glass ware 1) 2) approx. position of left knee	1) not recorded similar to grave 36 does not belong to this collection (p. 18)			
X(1-2)				
1) inside glass bowl (see glass ware 1) 2) inside glass bowl (see glass ware 1)				
a) (1-2) b) (1) c) (1-38)				
a) 1-2) near left side of neck of body do not belong to this collection (p. 17) b) 1) inside glass bowl (see glass ware 1) c) 1-38) inside glass bowl (see glass ware 1)				
X(1-3)				X(1-2)
1-3) near left side of pelvis of body				1-2) near pelvis of body
	1) broken spatula tested by dissolving oxide in H CL and found to be rolled copper plate flattened at one end			

TABLE II

	HIGHAM GRAVE 41	HIGHAM GRAVE 42	HIGHAM GRAVE 43
pottery a) decorated b) plain c) glazed	b) X(1)	c) X(1)	c) X(1)
location in grave	b) 1) immediately to right of head of body	c) 1) not recorded	c) 1) not recorded does not belong to this collection (p. 20)
glass ware			
location in grave			
utilitarian metal objects		X(1)	
location in grave		1) above right shoulder of body	
ivory objects			
location in grave			
decorative pieces a) metal b) ivory c) semi-precious stone d) varia		a) (1) (2-3) c) (5)	
location in grave		a) 1) on one of fingers of left hand of body 2-3) at right side of chest of body c) 5) on left side of body	
pinheads			
location in grave			
remarks	b) 1) fragment of splayed foot of drab greenish/brown clay, diam. foot ca. 0.06,3 m.; remaining height ca. 0.03 m.		

HIGHAM GRAVE 44	HIGHAM GRAVE 45	HIGHAM GRAVE 46	HIGHAM GRAVE 47
c) X(1)	c) X(1)	b) X(1-2)	
c) 1) at knees of body	c) 1) at feet of body	b) 1-2) near south wall of burial chamber	
		b) (?) c) (75) d) (1) (?)	
		b) various pieces inside alcove at south end of west wall of burial chamber c) 1-75) inside alcove at south end of west wall of burial chamber d) 1) idem ?) ostrich shells(?) idem	
		14 small skulls (perhaps of dogs) and numerous bones piled together in southernmost of the two alcoves. Also traces of broken red (some dark (black)) pottery	extensive traces of large, broken pottery, particularly in the east-west shaft of burial chamber

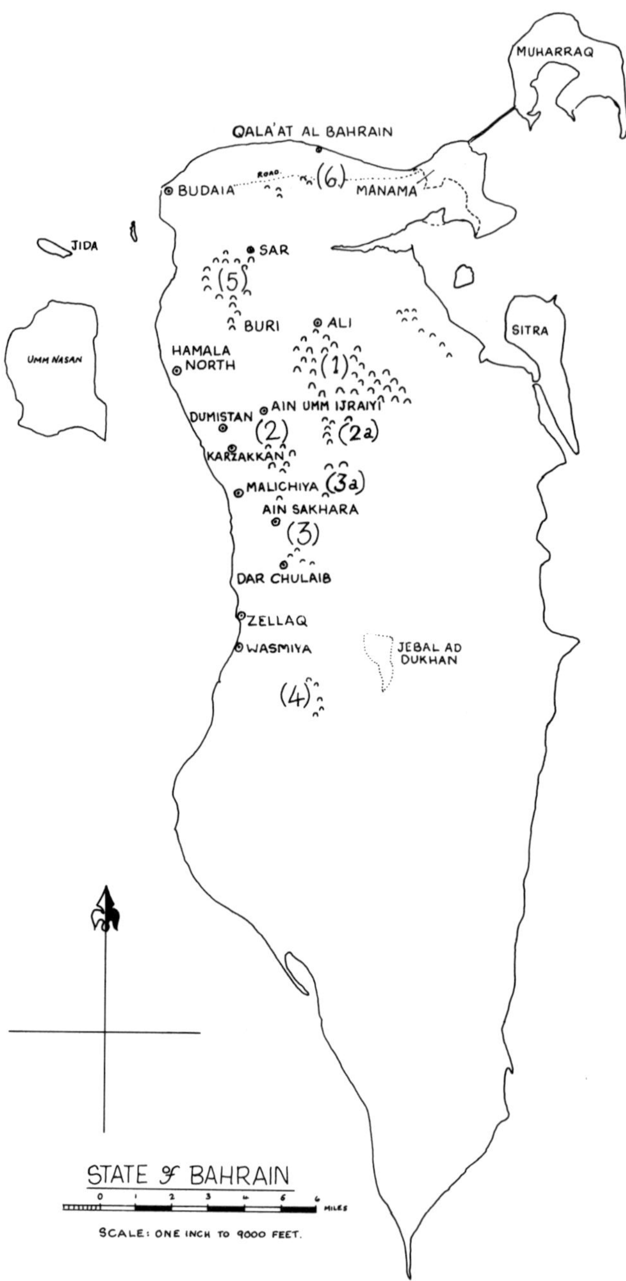

Fig. 1. Map of Bahrain Island showing the location of the recently excavated tumuli mentioned in the text. The semi circles represent areas of burial mounds.

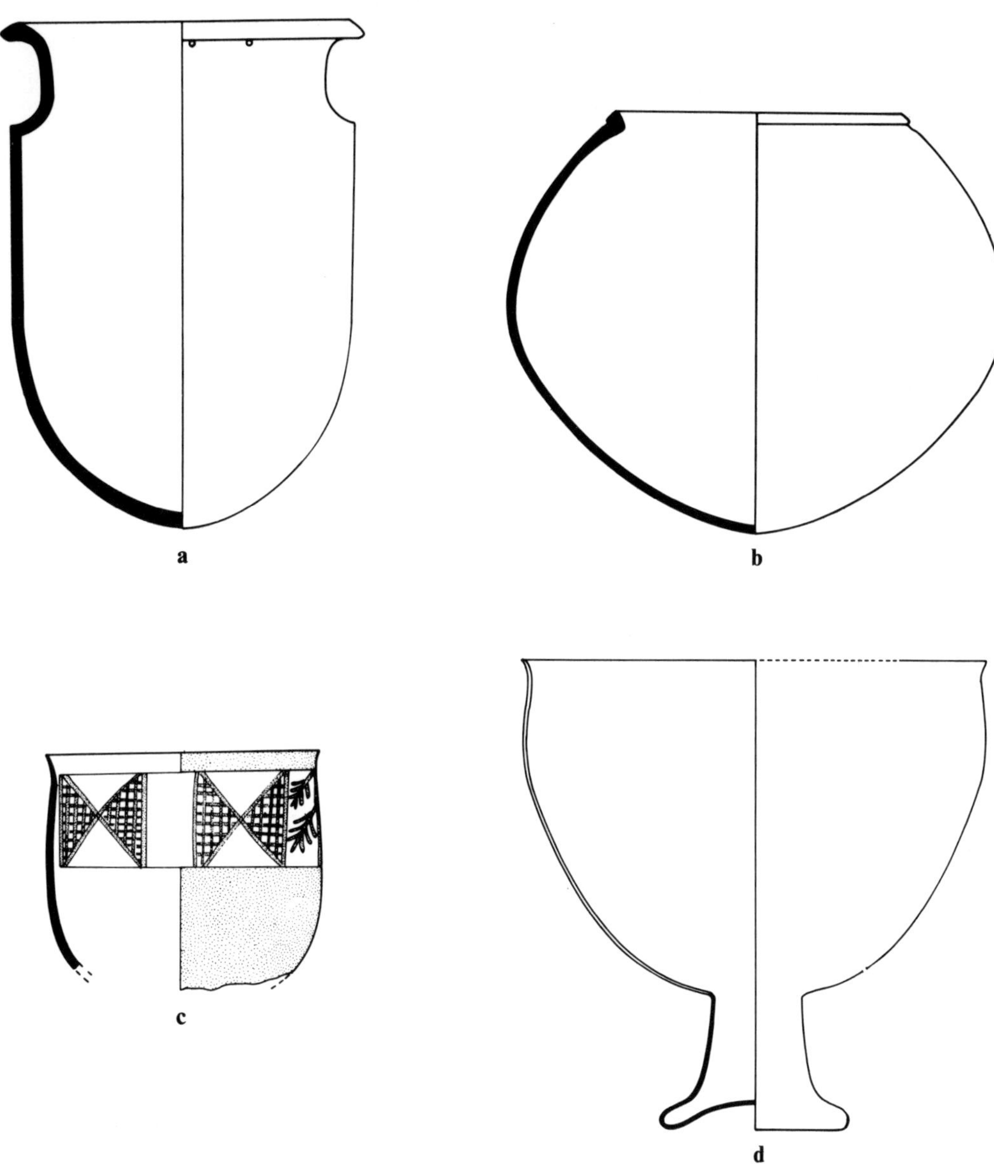

Fig. 2. Bahrain Island. Funerary pottery from the Jefferson grave mound at Hamala North (see Map Figure 1). By Courtesy of the Trustees of the British Museum, Department of Western Asiatic Antiquities.

a. B.M. 135130. Height 0.21 metres.
b. B.M. 135129. Height 0.17,1 metres.
c. B.M. 135131. Height 0.09,1 metres.
d. B.M. 135141. Height 0.18 metres.

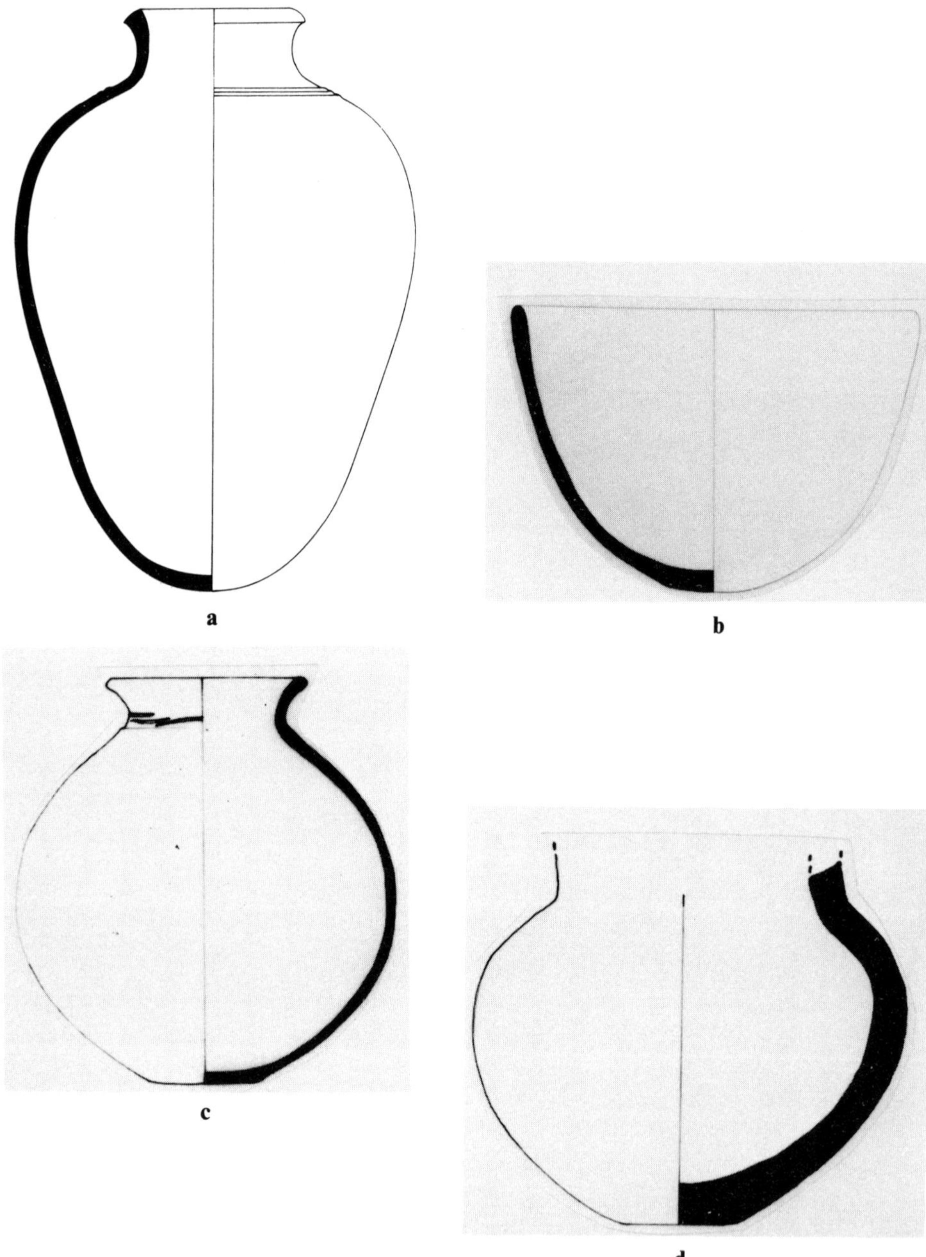

Fig. 3. Bahrain Island. Funerary pottery from the Jefferson grave mound (a), Higham grave 7 (b), Higham grave 23 (c) and Higham grave 27 (d). By Courtesy of the Trustees of the British Museum, Department of Western Asiatic Antiquities and Captain R. Higham.

a. B.M. 135128. Height 0.40,5 metres.
b. B.M. deposit no. 2693. Height 0.15 metres.
c. B.M. deposit no. 2693. Height 0.21 metres.
d. B.M. deposit no. 2693. Height 0.09 metres.

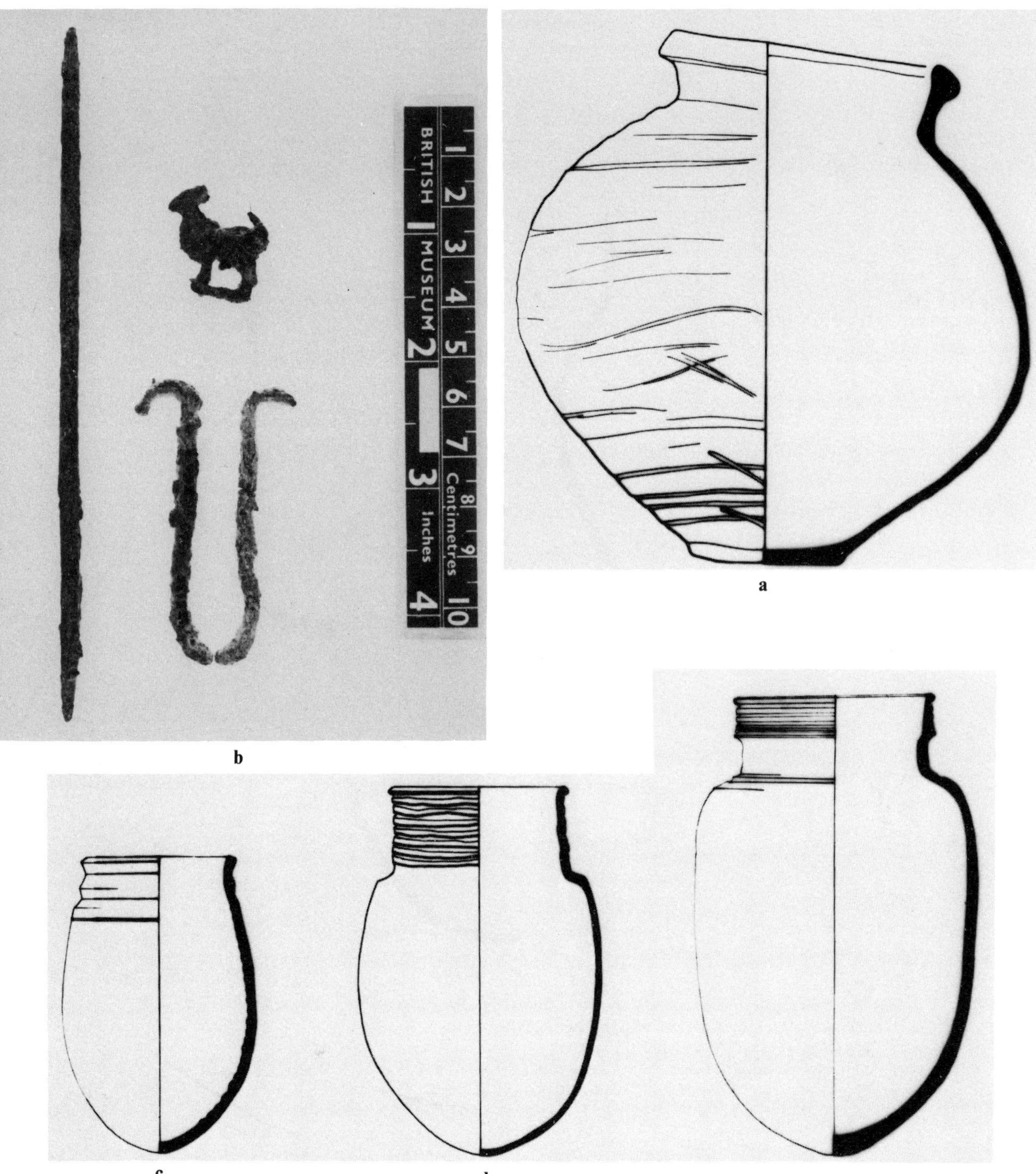

Fig. 4. Bahrain Island. Funerary pottery from Higham grave 32 (a), Jefferson grave mound (b), Higham grave 1 (c), Higham grave 7 (d), Higham grave 6 (e). By Courtesy of the Trustees of the British Museum, Department of Western Asiatic Antiquities and Captain R. Higham.

a. B.M. deposit no. 2693. Height 0.26 metres.

b. Pin B.M. 135137. Length 0.13,7 metres; "omega"-shaped pin(?) B.M. 135135. Length 0.05,7 metres; goat B.M. 135136. Height 0.02 metres.

c. B.M. deposit no. 2693. Height 0.15 metres.

d. B.M. deposit no. 2693. Height 0.18,5 metres.

e. B.M. deposit no. 2693. Height 0.23,4 metres.

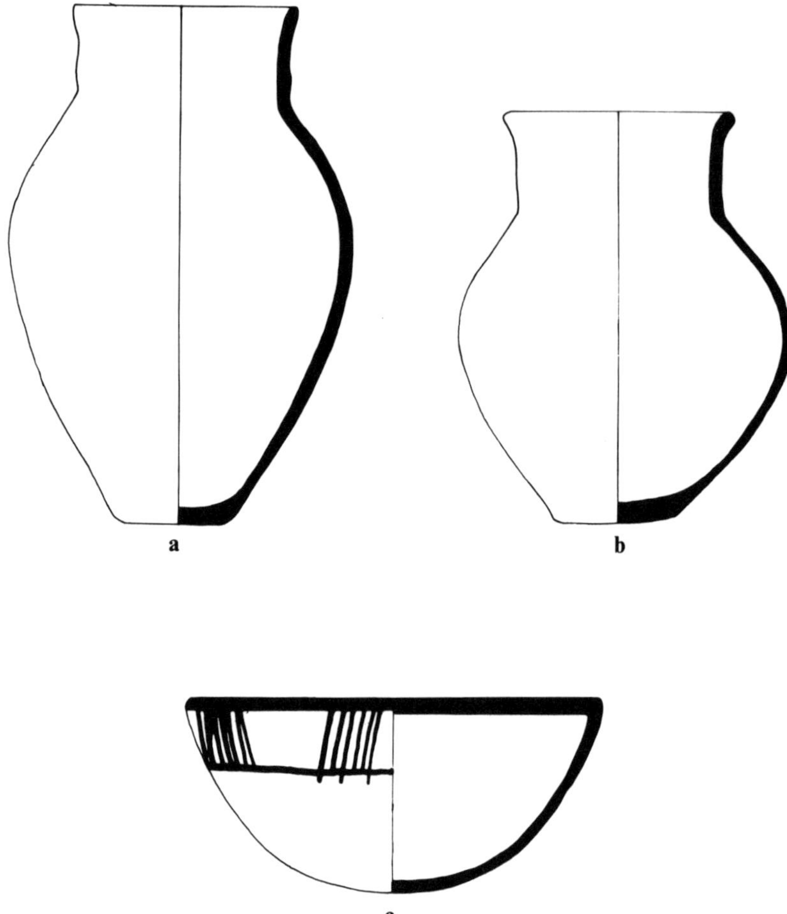

Fig. 5. Bahrain Island. Funerary pottery from Higham grave 5 (a), Higham grave 31 (b), Higham grave 7 (c). By Courtesy of Captain R. Higham.
a. B.M. deposit no. 2693. Height 0.20 metres.
b. B.M. deposit no. 2693. Height 0.16,1 metres.
c. B.M. deposit no. 2693. Height 0.07,5 metres.

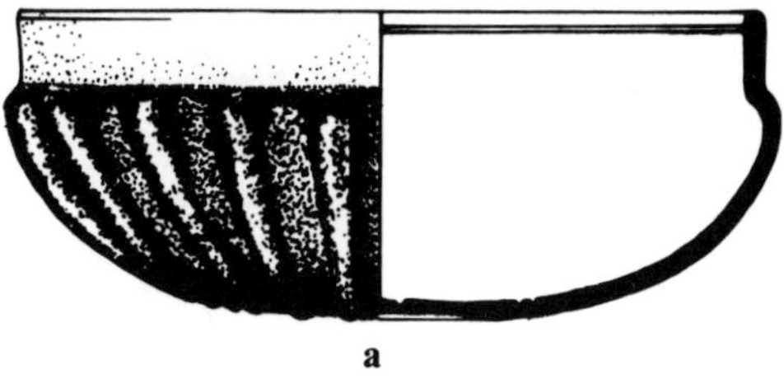

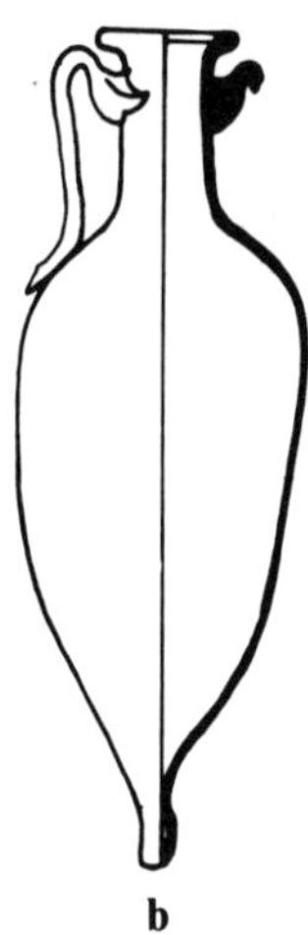

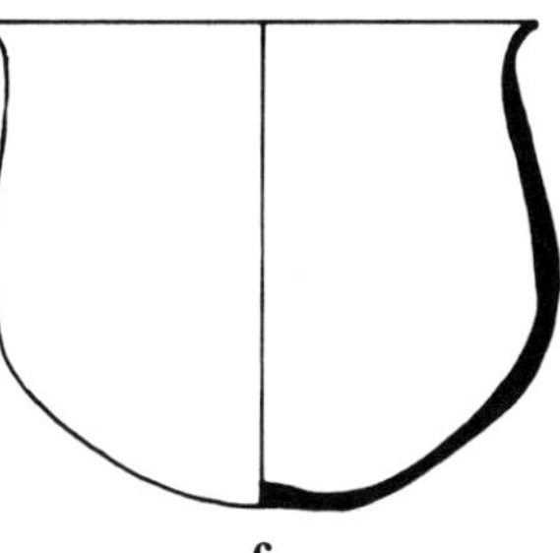

Fig. 6. Bahrain Island. Funerary pottery from Higham grave 36 (a-c). By Courtesy of Captain R. Higham.

a. B.M. deposit no. 2693. Height 0.04,6 metres.
b. B.M. deposit no. 2693. Height 0.12 metres.
c. B.M. deposit no. 2693. Height 0.06,3-0.06,6 metres.

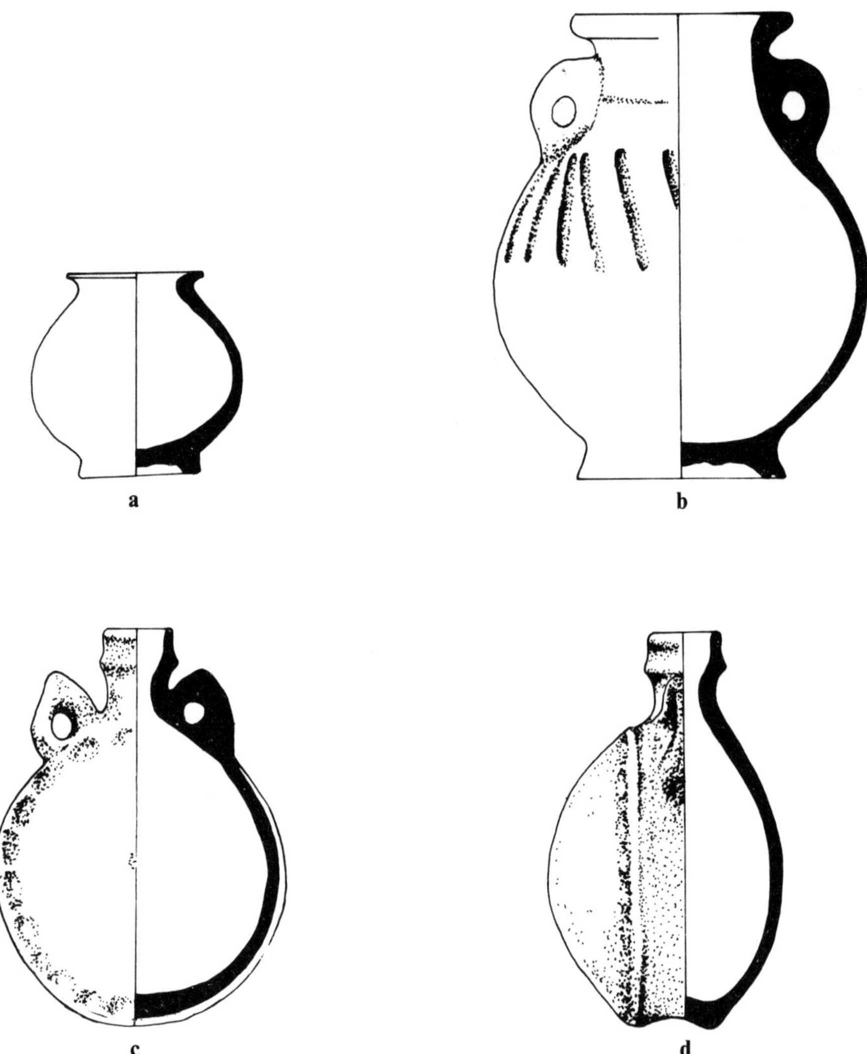

Fig. 7. Bahrain Island. Funerary pottery from Higham grave 36 (a, c-d), Higham grave 42 (b). By Courtesy of Captain R. Higham.

a. B.M. deposit no. 2693. Height 0.05,5 metres.
b. B.M. deposit no. 2693. Height 0.12,7-0.13,7 metres.
c-d. B.M. deposit no. 2693. Height 0.11 metres.

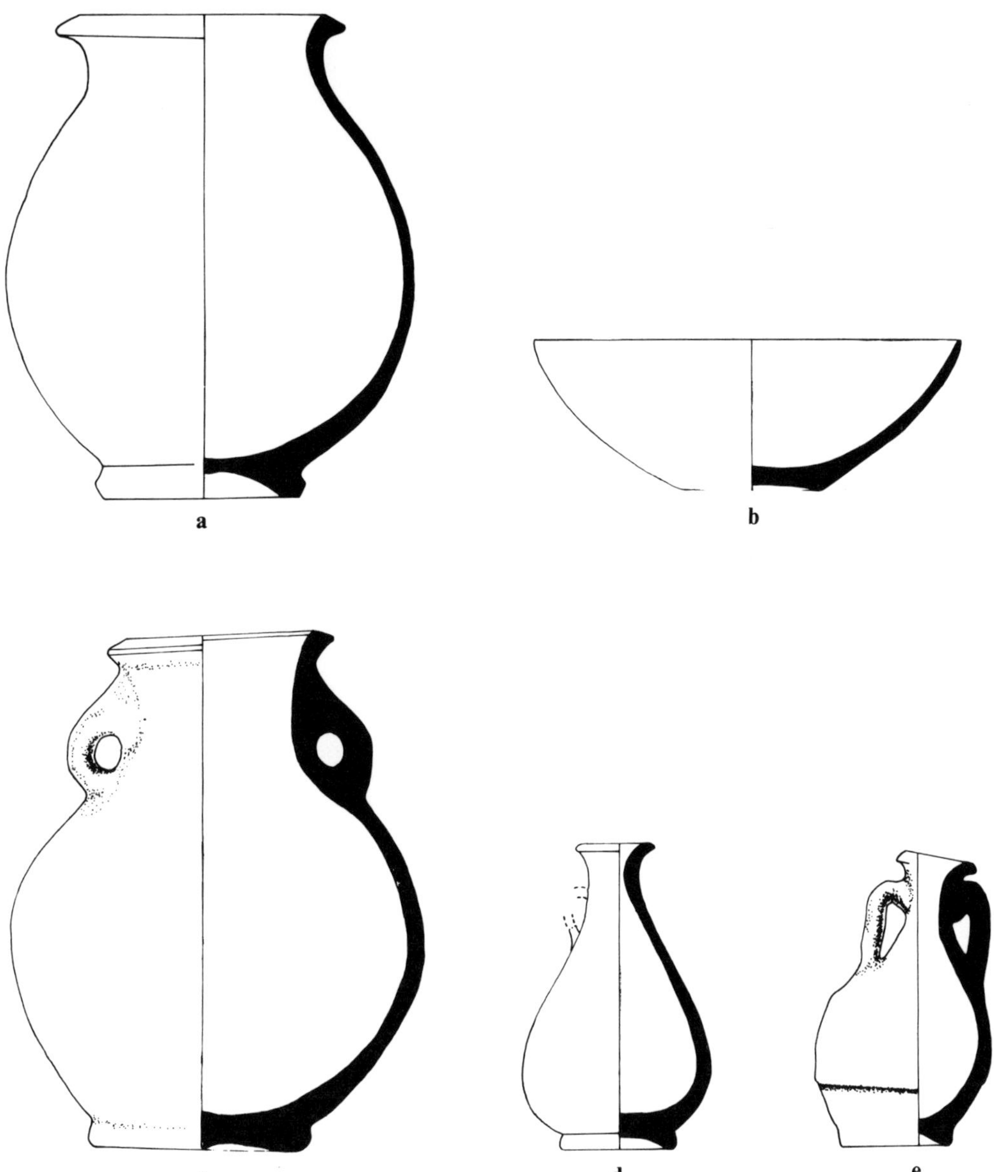

Fig. 8. Bahrain Island. Funerary pottery from Higham grave 39 (a), Higham grave 45 (b), Higham grave 40 (c), Higham grave 37 (d), Higham grave 44 (e). By Courtesy of Captain R. Higham.

a. B.M. deposit no. 2693. Height 0.17,5 metres.
b. B.M. deposit no. 2693. Height 0.05,3 metres.
c. B.M. deposit no. 2693. Height 0.19,4 metres.
d. B.M. deposit no. 2693. Height 0.10,3-0.10,8 metres.
e. B.M. deposit no. 2693. Height 0.10,8 metres.

PLATES

2

1

3

4

Bahrain Island. 1. Jefferson grave mound at Hamala North (see Map Figure 1). By Courtesy of Mrs. E.P. Jefferson. 2. Inside view of the Jefferson grave mound at Hamala North. By Courtesy of Mrs. E.P. Jefferson. 3-4. Higham grave mound south of the Portugese Fort and near the present Budaia-Manama road (graves 36-45) (see Map Figure 1, location 6). Photographs J.C.M.H. Moloney.

1 2 3 4

Bahrain Island. 1-4. Higham grave mound south of the Portugese Fort and near the present Budaia-Manama road (graves 36-45) (see Map Figure 1, location 6). Photographs J.C.M.H. Moloney.

1

2

Bahrain Island. Funerary pottery from the Jefferson grave mound at Hamala North (see Map Figure 1). By Courtesy of the Trustees of the British Museum, Department of Western Asiatic Antiquities. 1-2. B.M. 135129. Height 0.17,1 metres. Photographs British Museum (1) and C. May (2).

1

2

Bahrain Island. Funerary pottery from the Jefferson grave mound at Hamala North (see Map Figure 1). By Courtesy of the Trustees of the British Museum, Department of Western Asiatic Antiquities.

1. B.M. 135130. Height 0.21 metres. Photograph British Museum.
2. B.M. 135128. Height 0.40,5 metres. Photograph British Museum.

1

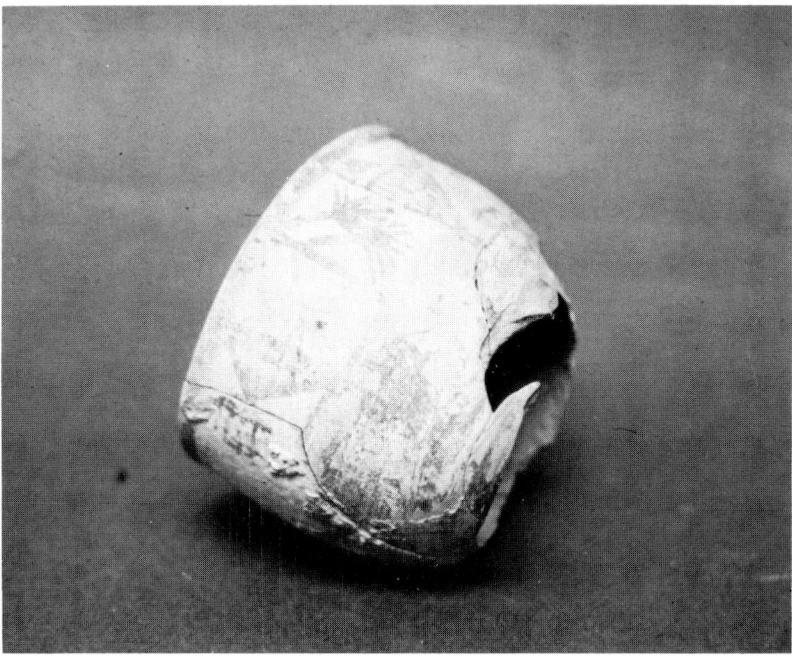

2

Bahrain Island. Funerary pottery from the Jefferson grave mound at Hamala North (see Map Figure 1). By Courtesy of the Trustees of the British Museum, Department of Western Asiatic Antiquities.
1-2. B.M. 135131. Height 0.09,1 metres. Photographs British Museum (1) and C. May (2).

1

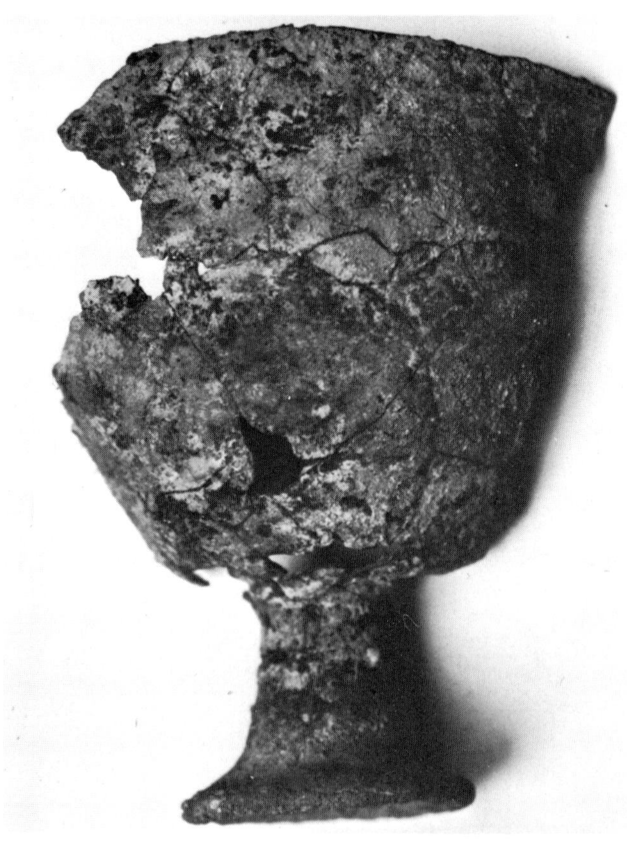

2

Bahrain Island. Funerary pottery from the Jefferson grave mound at Hamala North (see Map Figure 1). By Courtesy of the Trustees of the British Museum, Department of Western Asiatic Antiquities. 1-2. B.M. 135141. Height 0.18 metres. Photographs British Museum (1) and C. May (2).

1

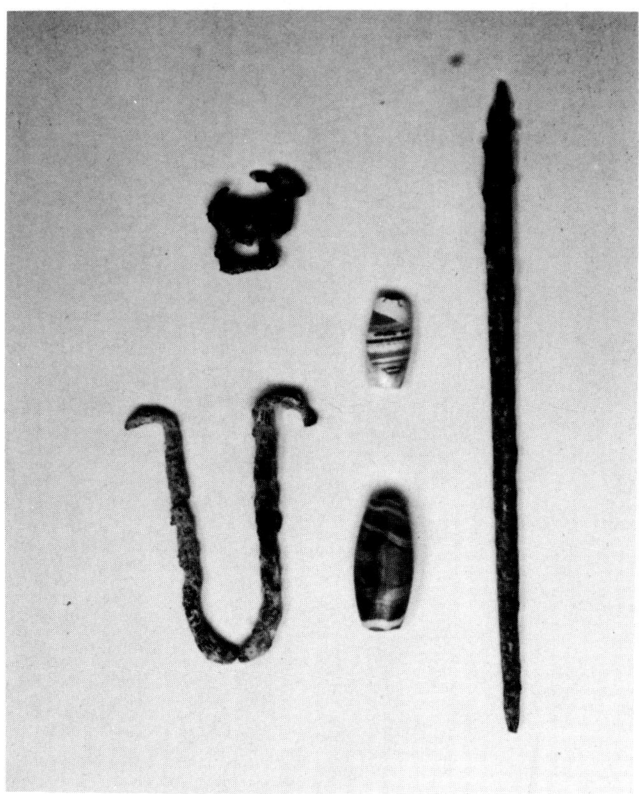

2

Bahrain Island. Funerary pottery from the Jefferson grave mound at Hamala North (see Map Figure 1). By Courtesy of the Trustees of the British Museum, Department of Western Asiatic Antiquities.
1. B.M. 135132. Diameter base 0.09,5 metres. Photograph British Museum.
2. Pin B.M. 135137. Length 0.13,7 metres; "omega"-shaped pin(?) B.M. 135135. Length 0.05,7 metres; goat B.M. 135136. Height 0.02 metres; larger agate bead B.M. 135138. Length 0.02,7 metres; smaller agate bead B.M. 135139. Length 0.01,8 metres. Photograph C. May.

1

2

Bahrain Island. Funerary pottery from Higham grave 1. By Courtesy of Captain R. Higham. 1-2. B.M. deposit no. 2693. Height 0.15 metres. Photographs J.C.M.H. Moloney.

1

Bahrain Island. Funerary pottery from Higham grave 1. By Courtesy of Captain R. Higham. B.M. deposit no. 2693. Height 0.15 metres. Photograph C. May.

1

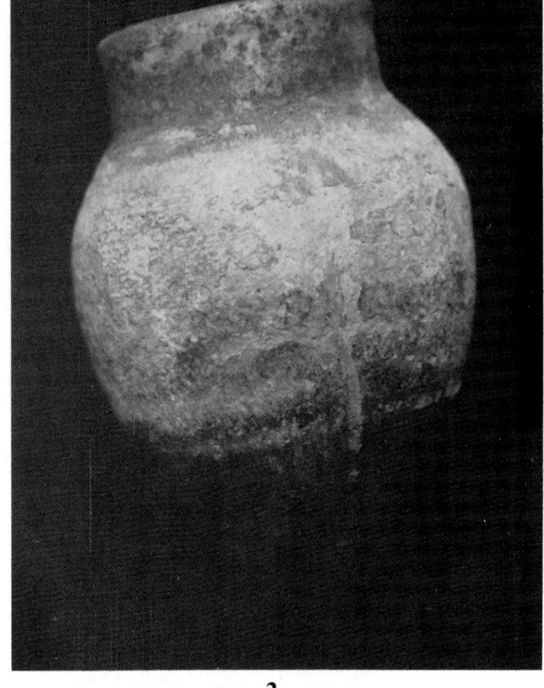

2

3

Bahrain Island. Funerary pottery from Higham grave 5. By Courtesy of Captain R. Higham. 1-3. B.M. deposit 2693. Height 0.20 metres. Photographs J. C. M. H. Moloney.

1

Bahrain Island. Funerary pottery from Higham grave 5. By Courtesy of Captain R. Higham. B.M. deposit no. 2693. Height 0.20 metres. Photograph C. May.

1

2

Bahrain Island. Funerary pottery from Higham grave 31. By Courtesy of Captain R. Higham. 1-2. B.M. deposit no. 2693. Height 0.16,1 metres. Photographs J. C. M. H. Moloney (1) and C. May (2).

1

2

Bahrain Island. Funerary pottery from Higham graves 5 & 31. By Courtesy of Captain R. Higham.
1. B.M. deposit no. 2693. Height 0.16,1 metres. Photograph C. May.
2. B.M. deposit no. 2693. Left height 0.16,1 metres, right height 0.20 metres. Photograph C. May.

1

2

Bahrain Island. Funerary pottery from Higham grave 6. By Courtesy of Captain R. Higham. 1-2. B.M. deposit no. 2693. Height 0.23,4 metres. Photographs J.C.M.H. Moloney (1) and C. May (2).

1

2

Bahrain Island. Funerary pottery from Higham grave 7. By Courtesy of Captain R. Higham.
1-2. B.M. deposit no. 2693. Height 0.18,5 metres. Photographs C. May (1) and J. C. M. H. Moloney (2).

1

2

Bahrain Island. Funerary pottery from Higham grave 7. By Courtesy of Captain R. Higham.
1-2. B.M. deposit no. 2693. Height 0.07,5 metres. Photographs C. May (1) and J. C. M. H. Meloney (2).

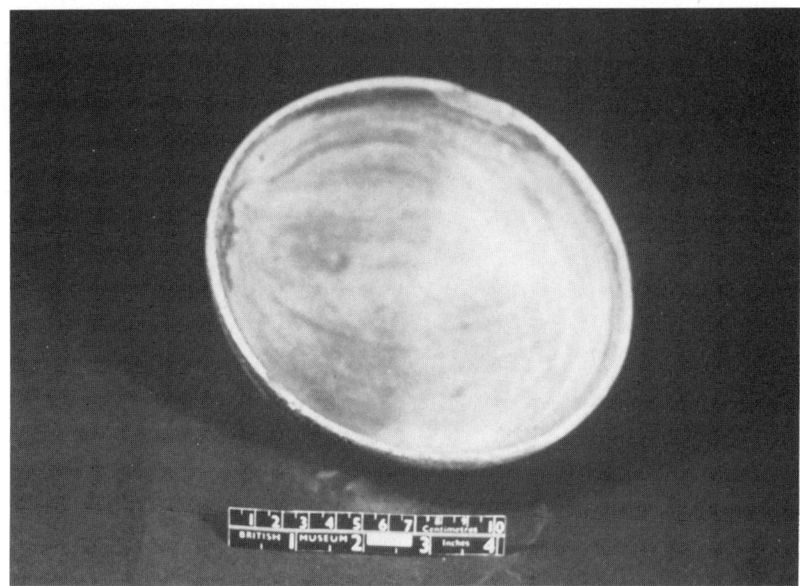

1

2

Bahrain Island. Funerary pottery from Higham grave 7 (1), Higham grave 7 (2). By Courtesy of Captain R. Higham.

1. B.M. deposit no. 2693. Height 0.07,5 metres. Photograph J. C. M. H. Moloney.
2. B.M. deposit no. 2693. Height 0.15 metres. Photograph C. May.

1

2

Bahrain Island. Funerary pottery from Higham grave 7 (1), Higham grave 7 (2). By Courtesy of Captain R. Higham.

1. B.M. deposit no. 2693. Height 0.15 metres. Photograph J. C. M. H. Moloney.
2. B.M. deposit no. 2693. See Plates XV-XVII. Photograph C. May.

1

2

Bahrain Island. Funerary pottery from Higham grave 11 (1), Higham grave 23 (2). By Courtesy of Captain R. Higham.

1. No information available. Photograph Captain R. Higham.
2. B.M. deposit no. 2693. Height 0.21 metres. Photograph C. May.

1

2

3

Bahrain Island. Funerary pottery from Higham grave 23 (1), Higham grave 27 (2-3). By Courtesy of Captain R. Higham.
1. B.M. deposit no. 2693. Height 0.21 metres. Photograph J. C. M. H. Moloney.
2-3. B.M. deposit no. 2693. Height 0.09 metres. Photographs C. May (2), J. C. M. H. Moloney (3).

1

2

Bahrain Island. Funerary objects from Higham grave 30 (1), Higham grave 32 (2). By Courtesy of Captain R. Higham.

1. B.M. deposit no. 2693. Length 0.12,9 metres. Photograph J.C.M.H. Moloney.
2. B.M. deposit no. 2693. Height 0.26 metres. Photograph J.C.M.H. Moloney.

1

2

Bahrain Island. Funerary pottery from Higham grave 32. By Courtesy of Captain R. Higham. 1-2. B.M. deposit no. 2693. Height 0.26 metres. Photographs J. C. M. H. Moloney.

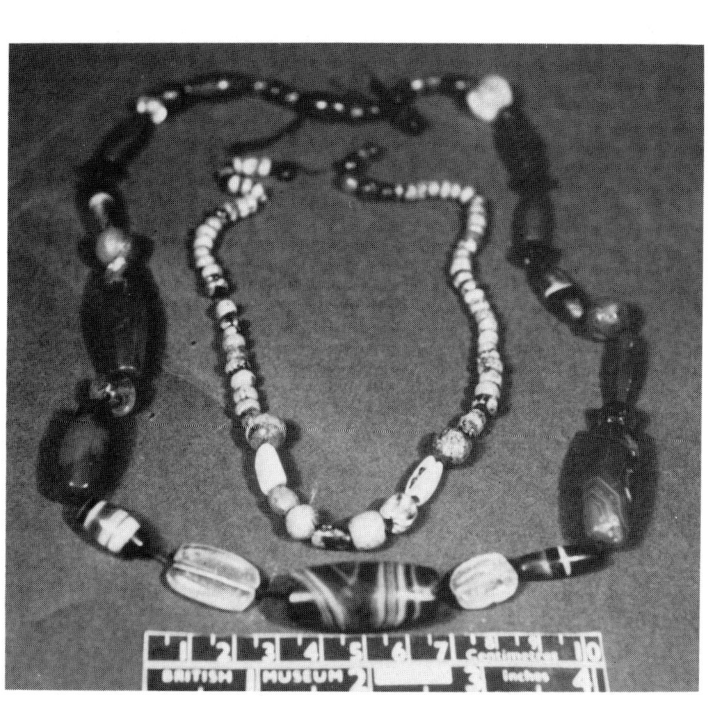

1

2

3

4

Bahrain Island. Funerary objects from Higham grave 46+36 (1), Higham grave 46 (2-4). By Courtesy of Captain R. Higham.

1. B.M. deposit no. 2693. Photograph J.C.M.H. Moloney.
2. B.M. deposit no. 2693. Photograph C. May.

3-4. B.M. deposit no. 2693. Measurements 0.01,1 × 0.02,7 metres. Photographs J.C.M.H. Moloney.

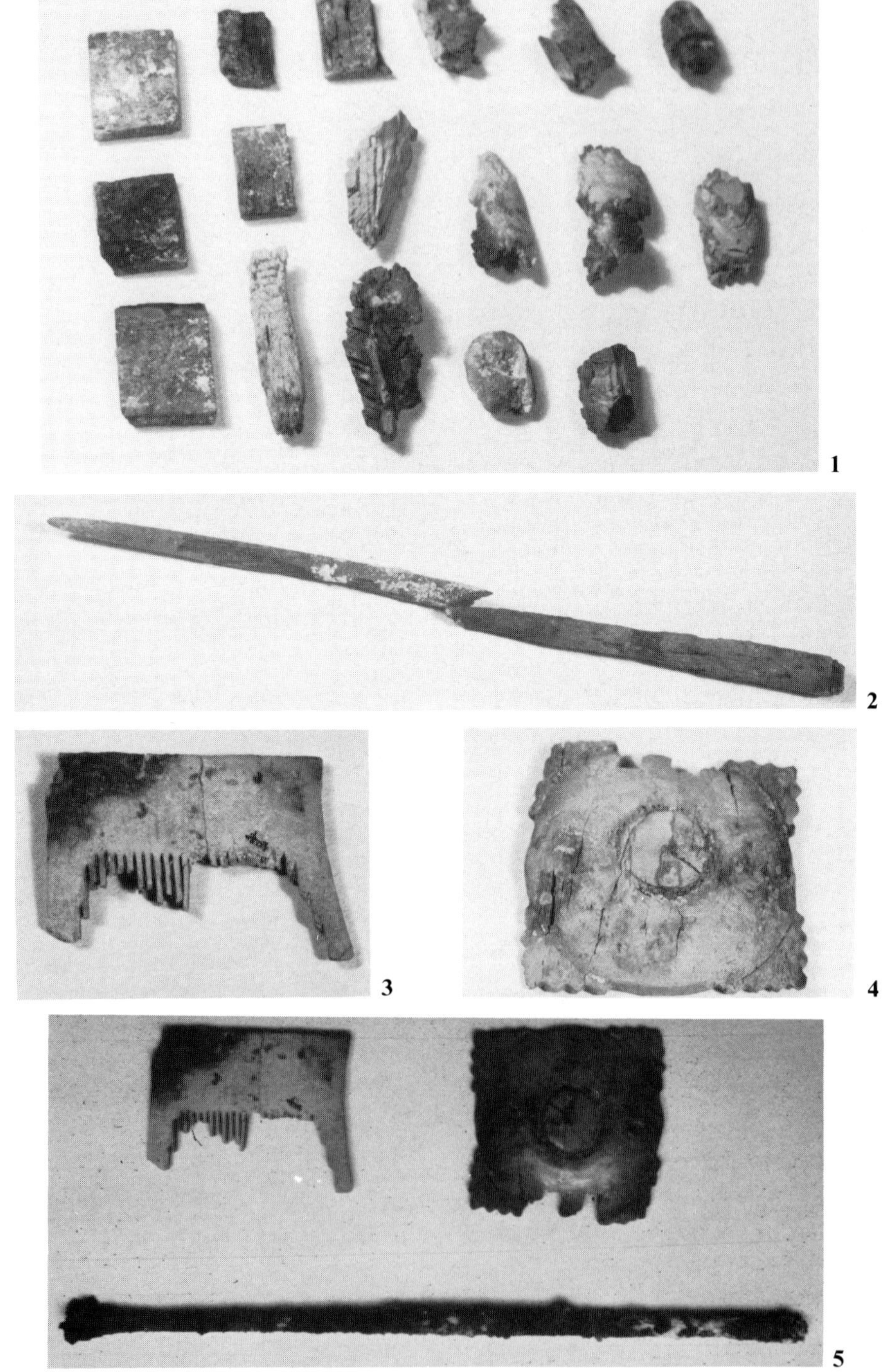

Bahrain Island. Funerary objects from Higham grave 46 (1), Higham grave 36 (2-5). By Courtesy of Captain R. Higham.

1. B.M. deposit no. 2693. Photograph J. C. M. H. Moloney.
2. B.M. deposit no. 2693. Length 0.15 metres. Photograph J. C. M. H. Moloney.
3. B.M. deposit no. 2693. Measurements 0.04 × 0.03,1 metres. Photograph J. C. M. H. Moloney.
4. B.M. deposit no. 2693. Measurements 0.03,8 × 0.03,8 metres. Photograph J. C. M. H. Moloney.
5. B.M. deposit no. 2693. Spatula length 0.15,4 metres. Other two objects see nos. 3-4. Photograph C. May.

1

2

Bahrain Island. Funerary glass bowl from Higham grave 36 (1-2). By Courtesy of Captain R. Higham.
1-2. B.M. deposit no. 2693. Height 0.04,6 metres. Photographs J. C. M. H. Moloney.

1

2

Bahrain Island. Funerary glass bowl from Higham grave 36 (1-2). By Courtesy of Captain R. Higham.
1-2. B.M. deposit no. 2693. Height 0.04,6 metres. Photographs J. C. M. H. Moloney.

1

2

3

Bahrain Island. Funerary glass cup from Higham grave 36 (1-3). By Courtesy of Captain R. Higham.
1-3. B.M. deposit no. 2693. Height 0.06,3-0.06,6 metres. Photographs C. May (1) and J. C. M. H. Moloney (2-3).

1

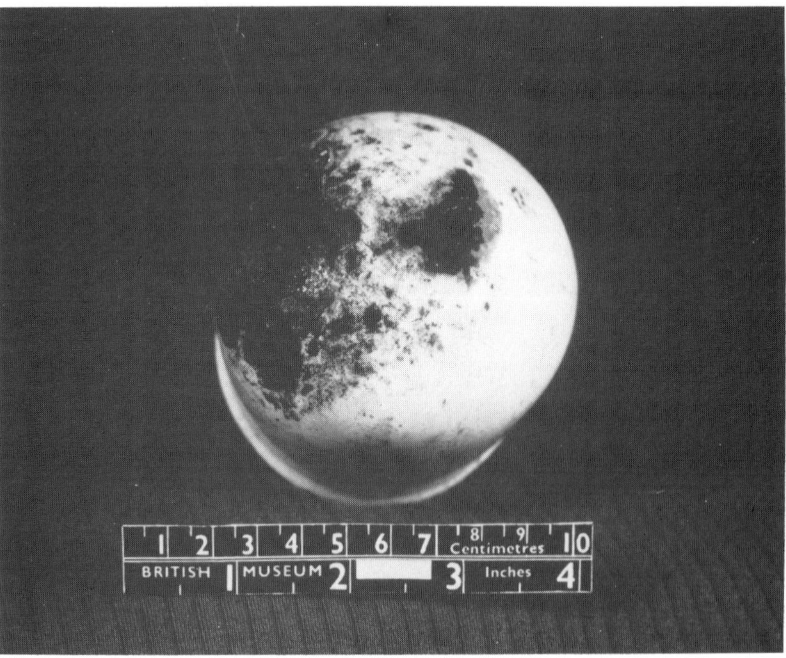

2

Bahrain Island. Funerary glass cup from Higham grave 36 (1-2). By Courtesy of Captain R. Higham. 1-2. B.M. deposit no. 2693. Height 0.06,3-0.06,6 metres. Photographs J. C. M. H. Moloney.

1

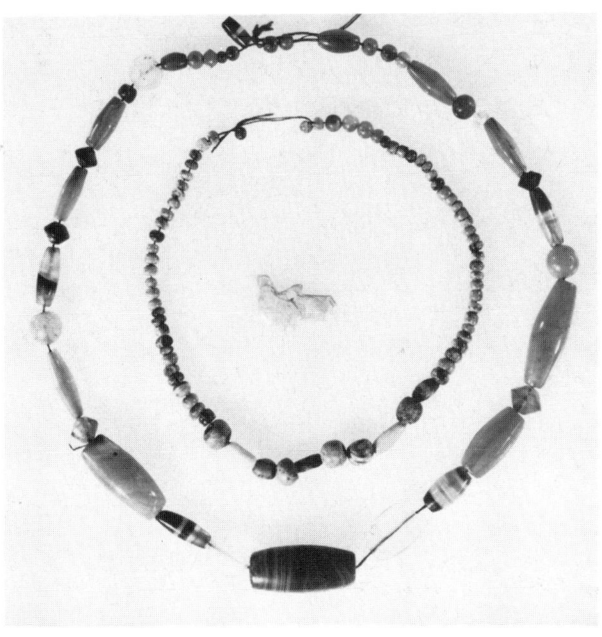

2

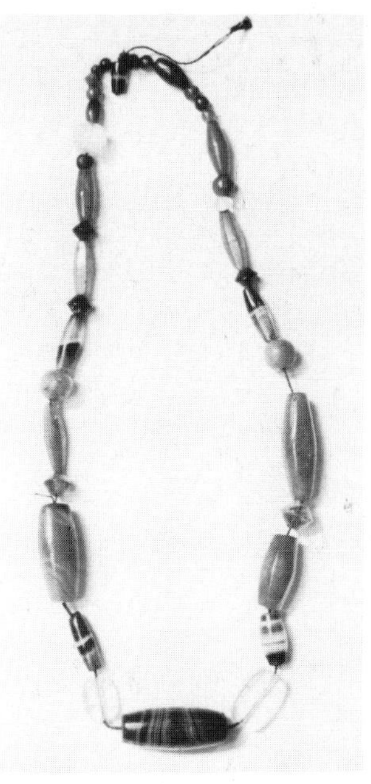

3

Bahrain Island. Funerary objects from Higham grave 36 (1, 2, 3), Higham grave 46 (2). By Courtesy of Captain R. Higham.
1. B.M. deposit no. 2693. Height 0.12 metres. Photograph C. May.
2-3. B.M. deposit no. 2693. See Plate XXIII 1-4. Photograph C. May.

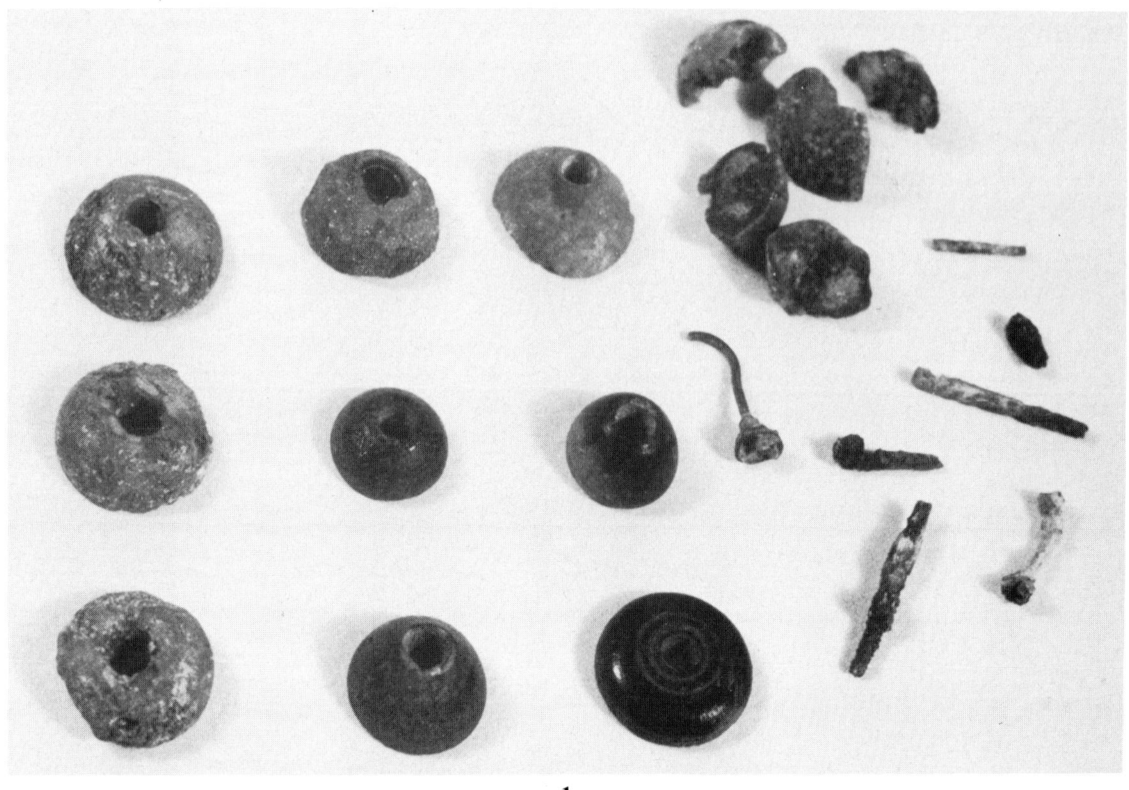

1

2

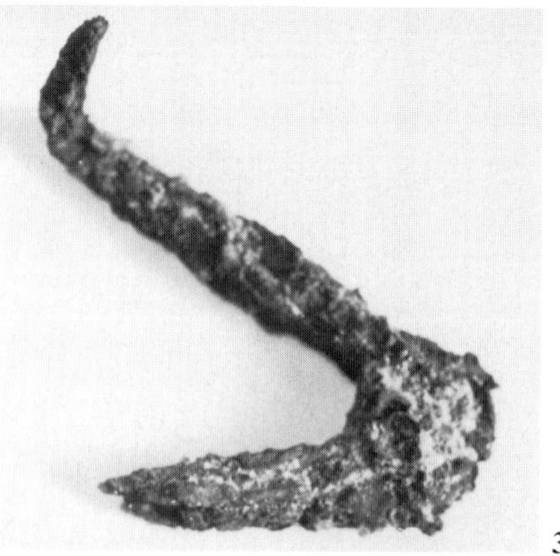

3

4

Bahrain Island. Funerary objects from Higham grave 36 (1-4), Higham grave 40 (1-2), Higham grave 42 (2). By Courtesy of Captain R. Higham.

1. B.M. deposit no. 2693. Photograph J.C.M.H. Moloney.
2. B.M. deposit no. 2693. See Plate XL 1-2. Photograph C. May.
3. B.M. deposit no. 2693. Length ca. 0.06,35 metres. Photograph J.C.M.H. Moloney.
4. B.M. deposit no. 2693. Length 0.15,4 metres. Photograph J.C.M.H. Moloney.

1

2

Bahrain Island. Funerary pottery from Higham grave 36 (1-2). By Courtesy of Captain R. Higham.
1-2. B.M. deposit no. 2693. Height 0.11 metres. Photograph J. C. M. H. Moloney.

1

Bahrain Island. Funerary pottery from Higham grave 36. By Courtesy of Captain R. Higham. B.M. deposit no. 2693. Height 0.11 metres. Photograph C. May.

1

2

3

Bahrain Island. Funerary pottery from Higham grave 36 (1-3), Higham grave 45 (3). By Courtesy of Captain R. Higham.
1-2. B.M. deposit no. 2693. Height 0.05,5 metres. Photographs C. May (1), J. C. M. H. Moloney (2).
3. B.M. deposit no. 2693. See Plates XXXI 1-2, XXXII, XXXIII 1-2. Photograph C. May.

1

2

3

Bahrain Island. Funerary pottery from Higham grave 37 (1-3). By Courtesy of Captain R. Higham.
1-3. B.M. deposit no. 2693. Height 0.10,3-0.10,8 metres. Photographs C. May (1), J. C. M. H. Moloney (2-3).

1

2

Bahrain Island. Funerary pottery from Higham grave 39 (1-2). By Courtesy of Captain R. Higham.
1-2. B.M. deposit no. 2693. Height 0.17,5 metres. Photographs J. C. M. H. Moloney.

1

2

Bahrain Island. Funerary pottery from Higham grave 40 (1-2). By Courtesy of Captain R. Higham.
1-2. B.M. deposit no. 2693. Height 0.19,4 metres. Photographs J. C. M. H. Moloney (1), C. May (2).

1

2

Bahrain Island. Funerary pottery from Higham grave 42 (1-2). By Courtesy of Captain R. Higham. 1-2. B.M. deposit no. 2693. Height 0.12,7-0.13,7 metres. Photographs J.C.M.H. Moloney.

1

Bahrain Island. Funerary pottery from Higham grave 42. By Courtesy of Captain R. Higham. B.M. deposit no. 2693. Height 0.12,7-0.13,7 metres. See Plates XXXVII 1-2, XXXIX 1-2. Photograph C. May.

1

2

Bahrain Island. Funerary pottery fnom Higham grave 39 (1-2), Higham grave 40 (1-2), Higham grave 42 (1-2). By Courtesy of Captain R. Higham.
1-2. B.M. deposit no. 2693. See Plates XXXV-XXXVIII. Photographs C. May.

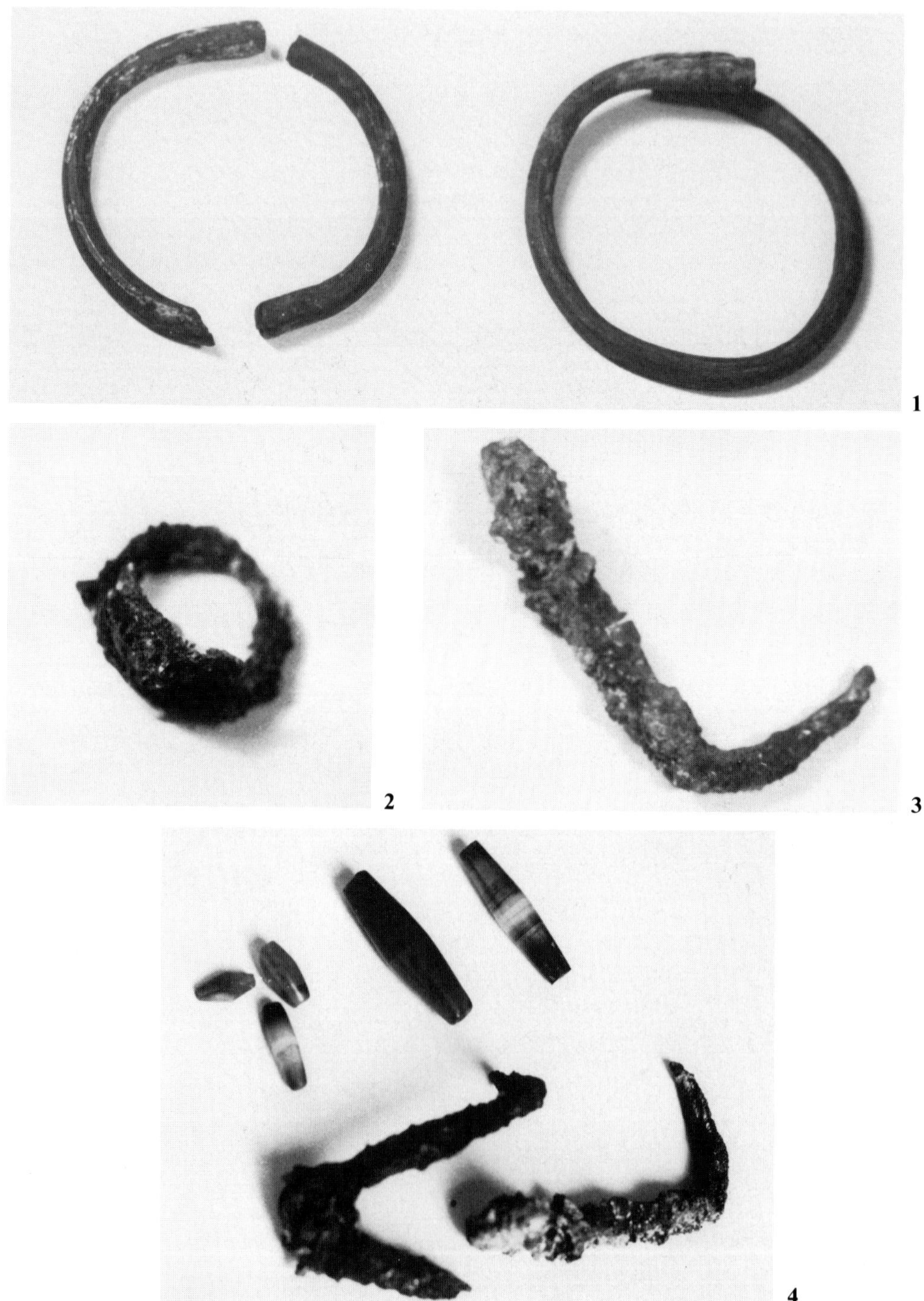

Bahrain Island. Funerary objects from Higham grave 36 (4), Higham grave 42 (1-4). By Courtesy of Captain R. Higham.

1. B.M. deposit no. 2693. Diameter of the right bangle 0.04,5 metres. Photograph J. C. M. H. Moloney.
2. B.M. deposit no. 2693. Diameter of ring ca. 0.02 metres. Photograph J. C. M. H. Moloney.
3. B.M. deposit no. 2693. Length ca. 0.05 metres. Photograph J. C. M. H. Moloney.
4. B.M. deposit no. 2693. Photograph J. C. M. H. Moloney.

1

2

3

Bahrain Island. Funerary pottery from Higham grave 37 (1), Higham grave 44 (1-3). By Courtesy of Captain R. Higham.

1. B.M. deposit no. 2693. Height left vase 0.10,8 metres; Height right vase 0.10,3-0.10,8 metres See Plate XXXIV 1-3. Photograph C. May.

2-3. B.M. deposit no. 2693. Height 0.10,8 metres. Photographs C. May (2), J.C.M.H. Moloney (3).

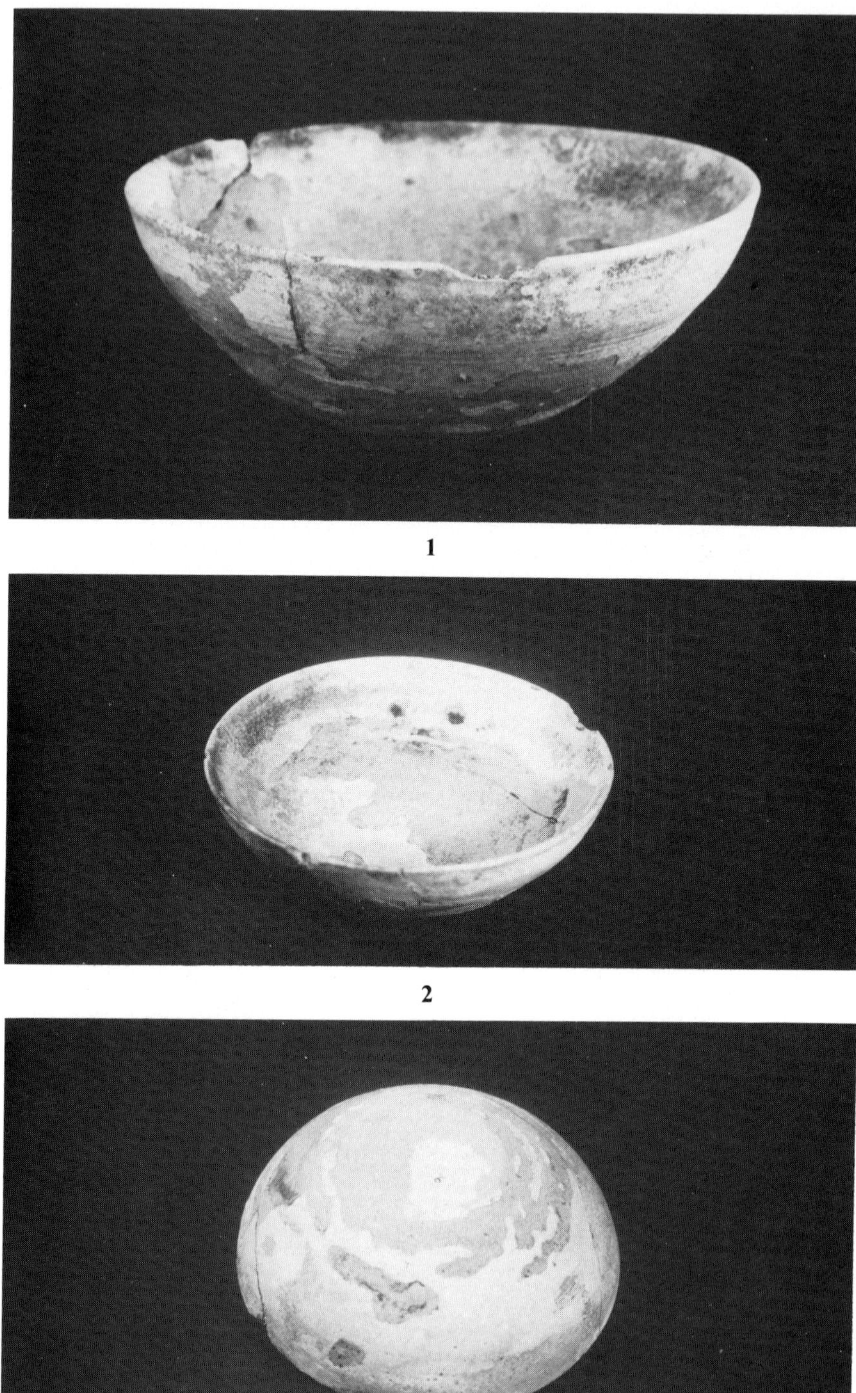

1

2

3

Bahrain Island. Funerary pottery from Higham grave 45 (1-3). By Courtesy of Captain R. Higham.
1-3. B.M. deposit no. 2693. Height 0.05,3 metres. See Plate XXXIII 3. Photographs C. May (1), J. C. M. H. Moloney (2-3).